THE
SCIENCE
OF
GROWTH

THE
SCIENCE
OF
GROWTH

HOW FACEBOOK BEAT FRIENDSTER—
AND HOW NINE OTHER STARTUPS
LEFT THE REST IN THE DUST

SEAN AMMIRATI

St. Martin's Press
New York

www.stmartins.com

Library of Congress Cataloging-in-Publication Data

Names: Ammirati, Sean, author.

Title: The science of growth : how Facebook beat Friendster—and how nine other startups left the rest in the dust / Sean Ammirati.

Description: New York : St. Martin's Press, 2016.

Identifiers: LCCN 2015045657| ISBN 9781250074294 (hardback) | ISBN 9781466885943 (e-book)

Subjects: LCSH: New business enterprises—Case studies. | Entrepreneurship—Case studies. | Management—Case studies. | Internet industry—Management—Case studies. | BISAC: BUSINESS & ECONOMICS / Entrepreneurship.

Classification: LCC HD62.5 .A48 2016 | DDC 658.1/1—dc23

LC record available at http://lccn.loc.gov/2015045657

Our books may be purchased in bulk for promotional, educational, or business use. Please contact your local bookseller or the Macmillan Corporate and Premium Sales Department at 1-800-221-7945, extension 5442, or by e-mail at MacmillanSpecialMarkets@macmillan.com.

Page design by Letra Libre

First Edition: April, 2016

10 9 8 7 6 5 4

CONTENTS

ACKNOWLEDGMENTS

FIRST, THIS BOOK WOULD NOT HAVE BEEN POSSIBLE WITHOUT THE SUP-port and encouragement of my wife, Jennifer. Thanks for understanding the weekends spent at the office writing, instead of out with you and our wonderful children.

I'd also like to thank my parents, Michael and Barbara. There are so many things I'll forever be grateful you taught me, but in this context thanks for demonstrating the significance of entrepreneurship.

To my mentor, Richard Florida, thanks for the encouragement to write this book and all your sage career advice over the years.

To my agent, Jim Levine, thanks for your wise and professional advice throughout the project. I'd also like to thank Emily Carleton and the entire team at St. Martin's Press. Emily, words can't express my gratitude for your detailed review and editorial assistance with this manuscript.

I would also like to thank all of my brilliant students from Carnegie Mellon. I learn as much from you as I teach. I'd especially like to thank Peter Schoffelen for his tireless and brilliant research, first as a student and later full-time on this project. I'd also like to thank my TA, Matt Crespi, for contributing to and synthesizing so much of the material here as well as keeping our classes organized and productive.

To Dave Mawhinney, for inviting me back to the Carnegie Mellon family as adjunct faculty. Dave, you are a wonderful friend and have impacted my career in so many ways going back to our first startup together—thank you.

Finally, to my partners at Birchmere, Sean Sebastian and Ned Renzi, it's an honor to work with you each day supporting great entrepreneurs.

FOREWORD

Richard Florida

IT'S A COMMONPLACE TO SAY THAT WE INHABIT A NEW ECONOMY. BUT WE do. The key to the old one was captured in Charles Wilson's oft-quoted phrase, "What's good for General Motors is good for the country" (which, like so many other benchmark sayings, was misquoted—what he really said was "for years I thought what was good for our country was good for General Motors, and vice versa"). Still, the gist of it was telling. The United States' economy revolved around giant, vertically integrated companies like GM and Ford, IBM and General Electric, US Steel and Proctor & Gamble. They powered the economy and their hundreds of thousands of employees spent the whole of their adult lives working for them. Cities measured their strength by how many of such companies' headquarters and manufacturing plants they had. Nobody ever even mentioned startup companies or the talent that drives them. You didn't have to scale anything, because the companies that mattered had such massive scale already.

The past several decades changed all that. Globalization hit hard at many once-great companies and deindustrialization decimated many of the great cities that housed them.

The driving force in our economy has shifted from those behemoths to smaller entrepreneurial startups—and even more importantly, to clusters of fast, nimble technology startups in places like Silicon Valley. Where the old economy was stable and centered, the new economy is more dynamic and volatile. In just the past decade or so, startups have been shifting away from the suburban nerdistans where they were traditionally incubated and toward the urban areas that the creative class has rediscovered and wants and needs to be. Downtown San Francisco now receives more venture capital than Silicon Valley proper; New York City attracts more venture capital than Boston and its surrounding Route 128 suburbs. Cities have the diversity of talent and industry, the density and interactive streetscapes, the openness to new ideas, and the fast-paced metabolisms that enable innovation and innovative enterprises to flourish.

As an urbanist, I've tried to codify a set of rules and best practices that city leaders and stakeholders can use to create quality, sustainable growth, based upon the simple notion that it is cities and the talent they attract that hold the key to prosperity. If a city is a place that can attract and retain talented, innovative people, innovative businesses will follow.

As a serial entrepreneur, a venture capitalist, and above all, a serious thinker, Sean Ammirati has been doing much the same thing for entrepreneurship and business startups. I've known him for a long time; the two of us first crossed paths when I was still a professor at Carnegie Mellon in Pittsburgh and when I was in the early stages of writing *Rise of the Creative Class.*

In *The Science of Growth,* he peers into the black box of successful startups, posing and answering the all-important question: What makes some startups scale quickly and others fail to take off at all? To get at it, he examines ten paired sets of companies to separate the winners and losers and identify what drives success—Facebook and Friendster in social media, for example, and McDonald's and White Castle in fast food—plus six other successful startups that were more or less unique, like Twitter, Airbnb, and Google.

What makes the difference? The answers Ammirati provides are powerful and complex. A key factor he zeros in on is the ability of companies to achieve "escape velocity." To my great delight and fascination, he shows that this is not an abstract construct but is a direct product of people and the places they inhabit. Successful startups reflect the passion and vision of the entrepreneurs who dream them up and bring them into the world, and the skills and technological prowess of the people who work for them.

At the same time, those entrepreneurs and their companies are products of the communities that they are embedded in, even as they in turn shape those places' long-term futures. "High-growth entrepreneurship is critical for a region's long-term health," Ammirati rightly points out, "new job growth is driven not by large corporations but by high-growth startups." When startups successfully scale, the places in which they are located often scale too. As more and more startups take root, a virtuous cycle sets in as other talented people and innovative companies are drawn to the city, generating more investment capital and improving its quality of place still more.

In *The Science of Growth*, Ammirati provides an essential playbook for the entrepreneurs and venture capitalists who are investing in and shaping the next round of disruptive, high-growth enterprises—and who are helping to power the future of our cities and of our economy as a whole.

Richard Florida, author of the best-selling The Rise of the Creative Class, *is the Director of the Martin Prosperity Institute at the University of Toronto's Rotman School of Management, Global Research Professor at NYU, and co-founder and editor-at-large of* The Atlantic's *CityLab.*

1

INTRODUCTION

"Genius is one percent inspiration and ninety-nine percent perspiration."

—Thomas Edison

IF SOMEONE AWOKE AFTER A FIFTY-YEAR SLUMBER, THEY'D FIND THE NEW
world to be a magical place. The phones in our pockets can call anyone in
the world, yet we rarely speak into them. Instead, they are fully functioning computers with "apps" that can make a car or meal show up magically
without our having to utter a word. If the modern-day Rip Van Winkle
were to open the paper (likely on a tablet), they could read about multiple
companies trying to build self-driving cars. Of course, prior generations
could point to advances in their lifetimes that were similarly transformative,
including the mass adoption of automobiles, televisions, radios, telephones,
and even electricity.

It's because of passionate entrepreneurs that each of these improvements
exists. Entrepreneurs see things that are broken in our everyday lives, and create the world they think we ought to live in by commercializing innovation.

I think the future is very bright, because more and more people are contemplating entrepreneurship as a career. From 1990 until today, the number
of entrepreneurship programs on college campuses has increased from 180
to over 2,000.[1] The quality of these programs and the entrepreneurs they
educate is a key point of differentiation for universities.[2]

And these emerging entrepreneurs have more and more high-quality material available to them, both in the classroom and on their nightstands. Thanks to thought leaders like Eric Reis and Steve Blank, the lean startup movement has captivated Silicon Valley and entrepreneurs across the country.

If you aren't familiar with the lean startup movement, it's a philosophy that basically takes the scientific method and applies it to the process of building a company. You devise a set of experiments, as efficiently as possible, to validate or invalidate key hypotheses about your business. The term "lean" comes from some of the techniques this process leverages from lean manufacturing.

I'm a big unapologetic fan of the lean startup movement, so much so that I teach the Lean Entrepreneurship graduate course at Carnegie Mellon University. I also work as a venture capitalist, helping companies early in their life cycle use many of these techniques to better understand their customers and build the right products for them.

One day, however, at the end of one of my lean entrepreneurship courses, a masters student in robotics and I were chatting on the way out of class. This student is brilliant, but to be honest, had also been a challenge throughout the course. He regularly asked questions that he knew would take the lecture in a completely different direction than I had planned, and it often caused me to have to play catch-up. If you think back to your time in school, you can probably recall at least one student like him.

Walking out of class that night, he complimented me on the course and said how much he had learned from it, describing it as "the best course [he'd] taken in his entire time at CMU." I was relieved, but only momentarily, as he followed up with, "But it was a waste of time." I paused, thought to myself, "All feedback is a gift," and asked him to elaborate.

He explained that while it was great to learn about the processes and techniques that can turn an idea into a product that solves a real problem in a good market (a startup goal often called "product-market fit"), a much more relevant question (and one that would go on to form the basis for this book) was: **What happens after you find product-market fit?**

The more I thought about it, the more profound the question actually seemed. It's certainly true that plenty of companies have ultimately failed because they never built a product that solved a real problem, at least not for a large enough market to build a viable business.

But there were plenty of other companies that did build a product that solved a real problem for customers, yet never achieved the scale their founders envisioned. For every success story, like Facebook, there are thousands of stories of companies that started strong, then faded. In fact, the night that student and I chatted, Facebook had just released another strong set of earnings results, and was exploding in aftermarket activity. Yet, as most people older than 35 can remember, Facebook was predated by a number of competing social networks—including Friendster—that ultimately stalled out.

As my mind started racing, I wondered, Why do some companies stall out while others scale up? Are there best practices and techniques, similar to those I had taught in my Lean Entrepreneurship course, that could help at this stage of hypergrowth?

I also came to appreciate that for many of my grad students—because of visa issues, educational loans, or career ambitions—how to scale up a company was actually a much more relevant topic than how to start one. At this point in their lives, many of them were planning to join a venture-backed startup and contribute to scaling it up, not to found one.

I decided to step back and create a complementary course that would focus on exactly this topic of hypergrowth. I started by searching for a text like Eric Reis's *Lean Startup* and Steve Blank's *Startup Owner's Manual* to serve as the foundation of the new course. However, while I found tons of great resources on specific aspects, such as how to market or finance your startup, there was no holistic framework—complete with best practices and vocabulary—on what to do *after* you've found product-market fit.

As I started pulling material for the course, I became frustrated that the narrative didn't easily fit together. A hodgepodge of different material from different books—sometimes with conflicting recommendations—wouldn't get the job done. So in collaboration with my graduate students at Carnegie Mellon, I led an exploration looking at 20 different companies, split into pairs, that had achieved product-market fit at about the same point in their histories and had the same general target customer—but in each pair, one company had gone on to achieve real scale, while the other languished, never realizing its full potential. We augmented our research with an additional six companies that did not have a clear peer, but had achieved tremendous scale using the best practices identified in our earlier research.

The startups that achieved scale not only generated great wealth for their founders and early investors but, just as important, changed the world. The ones that did not, did not. What was the difference that meant so much?

You could easily assume that it was luck, but you'd be wrong. While each company's approach is of course unique, I've discovered that there is a science to growth. Across these case studies, a set of best practices has emerged, which I summarize in this book.

OVERVIEW OF RESEARCH

One of the most common questions I get when talking to people about this book and earlier research is: How does this relate to *Good to Great* and *Built to Last* by Jim Collins?

First of all, I should say I'm a huge fan of all of Jim Collins's work. His books were some of the most influential I read as a young entrepreneur and inspired me to build my own startups. I hope that this work will be similarly inspiring to future entrepreneurs.

Like Collins's work, this book takes a pair-wise comparison approach to the case studies. I believe this is effective because it avoids an oversight that many business texts make—specifically, looking only at success stories and ignoring the many failed companies that took a similar approach.

However, this book's focus is exclusively on startups early in their development. When the students and I started looking for these pairs of companies, we didn't have a hard-and-fast set of rules to drive selection. We were interested in what these companies were doing long before they went public. In fact, some of the successful companies were ultimately acquired; others are still privately held. Certainly, the companies that failed never achieved any public offering. Therefore, there was no standardized financial reporting information available for all the companies we looked at, and we could not come up with a single set of financial performance rules to determine which companies to include and which to exclude from our study.

Instead, the students and I used relatively famous companies as examples, because, when conducting completely secondary research, it is helpful to have a lot of information to pull from. It also enabled us (and the reader of this book) to have a better understanding of what the companies do, since most of them make products we interact with in our everyday lives.

We also focused primarily, but not exclusively, on software and Internet companies. This was helpful in several ways. First, there is a lot of information available about such companies, especially at the early stages of their growth when they are still privately held. Additionally, most executives today are realizing that even if their company is more of an industrial company, they can't ignore the reality that software is transforming their industry. Recently on the *Charlie Rose* show, Jeff Immelt, the CEO of General Electric, commented:

> It's our belief that every industrial company, in the coming age, is also going to be a software and analytics company. The people that deny that digitization is going to impact every corner of the economy are going to get left behind.[3]

However, we didn't limit ourselves to these types of companies, as we wanted to make sure the principles were broadly applicable to all types of transformative innovations. One particularly interesting case was the development of Fisker and Tesla in their race to commercialize electric cars. One company has gone on to be worth more than $25 billion,[4] while the other filed for bankruptcy.

As any executive can tell you, the rate of change has accelerated dramatically over the last few decades, the time frame in which almost all of our chosen companies were established. However, for historical perspective, we've analyzed the case of McDonald's versus White Castle, two companies founded in the first half of the twentieth century. In fact, White Castle was started almost 20 years before McDonald's and invented the kitchen assembly line that McDonald's later popularized. McDonald's took advantage of many of the best practices later used by Internet companies like Facebook and Tumblr and today has over 34,000 locations, while White Castle has less than 500.

The full set of companies analyzed follows in the tables below:

TABLE 1.1

Company	Founded	Product/Market Overview	Outcome
Tumblr	2/2007	Simple, lightweight online publishing	Acquired by Yahoo! for $1.1B in 5/2013
Posterous	5/2008		Acquired by Twitter for $10M
Tesla	7/2003	Electric cars	IPO in 7/2010 and currently valued at more than $27B
Fisker	8/2007		Declared bankrupt in 11/2013
Mint	11/2006	Online personal finance software	Acquired by Intuit for $170M in 9/2009
Wesabe	12/2005		Shut down in 6/2010
Automattic (WordPress)	7/2005	Blogging platform	Still privately held; used by over 60M sites on the Internet
Six Apart (Movable Type)	5/2003		No forward development since 2011 and merged with VideoEgg to form SAY Media
YouTube	2/2005	Online video-sharing platform	Sold to Google for $1.5B
Revver	10/2004		Sold to Live Universe for $5 M; shut down in 3/2011
Facebook	2/2004	Social network	IPO in 5/2012; currently valued at over $270B
Friendster	1/2001		Acquired by MOL Global for $26.4M in 12/2009
LinkedIn	5/2003	Professional social network	IPO in 7/2011 and currently valued at $25B; according to Quantcast, gets 75 million US visitors per month to site
Spoke	1/2002		Still privately held; according to Quantcast, gets less than 200K visitors per month to site
Hotmail	7/1996	Web-based e-mail provider	Sold to Microsoft for $400M in 12/1997
Juno	5/1996		Merged with NetZero and rolled into United Online
Cvent	1/1999	Cloud-based event management	Went public in 7/2013 and currently valued at $1.3B
StarCite	1/1998		Acquired by Active Networks for $51M in 12/2010
McDonald's	5/1940	Fast-food kitchen assembly line for hamburgers	Currently valued at $97B with more than 34,000 locations
White Castle	9/1921		Privately held with less than 500 locations

(For more details on these companies, please see Appendix.)

TABLE 1.2

Company	Founded	Product/Market Overview	Outcome
Google	9/1998	Online search engine	Went public in 8/2004 and currently valued at $455B
PayPal	12/1998	Online payment and money transfer	Acquired by eBay for $1.5B in 7/2002
Twitter	3/2006	Real-time short update communication platform	Currently valued at $21B
Dropbox	6/2007	Online cloud storage	Still privately held but, according to multiple press reports, raised $350M, most recently (Q1 2014) at a $10B valuation[5]
Airbnb	8/2008	Marketplace of places of short-term rental opportunities	Still privately held but current speculation in the *Wall Street Journal* is a valuation of $24B[6]
Uber	3/2009	Marketplace connecting riders with transportation options; originally focused on black car service.	Still privately held but current speculation in the *Wall Street Journal* is a valuation of over $50B[7]

MORE DETAILS ON THE COMPANIES CHOSEN

If you are already familiar with all of the companies chosen, you can skip this section. If not, you can jump to the companies with which you are not acquainted.

Tumblr and Posterous

Both Tumblr and Posterous provided a microblogging solution. The idea of a microblog is to provide a web platform on which individuals can publish short and frequent updates. As the name implies, the service is optimized for shorter updates relative to what you might typically think of from a traditional blog. This content typically includes photos, quotes, or very short (usually less than a few paragraphs) text updates. Tumblr was launched in February 2007 and about five years later was acquired by Yahoo for $1.1 billion. Today (as of July 1, 2015) Tumblr hosts over 240 million blogs. Posterous was started shortly after Tumblr and was its main competitor in the early years of development, but unfortunately it never achieved similar scale. The company was eventually shut down on March 12, 2012, after the majority of its team was acquired by Twitter in what has become known as an "acqui-hire" (in which the purpose of the transaction is not primarily to acquire the startup's technology or customer base, but its team).

Tesla and Fisker

Tesla Motors and Fisker Automotive both sought to create a premium *electric* car for mass production. Tesla would ultimately fulfill that vision—first with a sports car (Tesla Roadster), later with a premium sedan (Tesla Model S), and most recently with a premium SUV (Tesla Model X). In the first quarter of 2015, Tesla delivered over 10,000 Model S vehicles to owners around the world. Fisker on the other hand would end up producing only one vehicle (Karma), whose production was suspended shortly before the company declared bankruptcy.

Mint and Wesabe

Mint and Wesabe were two free web-based personal finance management services. They both sought to make it easier for individuals to manage personal finances by tracking bank, credit card, investment, and loan transactions and balances as well as making budgets and setting goals. Mint grew rapidly and was eventually purchased by Intuit, the maker of Quicken and TurboTax. Wesabe launched in December 2005, a full ten months before Mint. Despite this early lead, Wesabe failed to gain significant market share and ultimately was shut down after running out of money.

Automattic (WordPress) and Six Apart (Movable Type)

Automattic and Six Apart both provided a service for hosting blogs. A unique aspect of these companies is they both were built around software that their founders had created to manage blogs. In the case of Automattic, that blogging software was WordPress; for Six Apart it was Movable

Type. The companies the two entrepreneurs founded simplified the process of running this blogging software on the Internet. It's difficult to separate the blogging software from the companies; we'll highlight stories of both throughout the book. WordPress was launched in August 2005 and is now used by over 60 million sites, including more than 23.3 percent of the top ten million websites (as of January 2015). WordPress competed directly with Six Apart and its Movable Type blogging service, which was launched in 2001, well before WordPress. However, eventually WordPress overtook Movable Type as the preferred blogging platform, and today almost no one uses Movable Type. Automattic is a thriving company valued at over $1 billion in its last financing round. Six Apart, on the other hand, was merged with VideoEgg to form a new company, SAY Media, and less than three months later that new company sold the Movable Type assets to a Japanese IT services company.

YouTube and Revver

YouTube and Revver were both early entrants in creating an online video-sharing platform. YouTube was founded by three former PayPal employees in 2005. The site made it incredibly simple to upload, share, and watch videos. In 2006 Google purchased YouTube for $1.65 billion. Revver entered the video-sharing market with a product similar to YouTube but with what they believed was a better solution: They attached advertising to all videos uploaded to their site and offered to share ad revenue with content creators. Unfortunately for the three founders of Revver, this differentiation didn't result in the same growth YouTube experienced. The company was acquired by LiveUniverse and eventually shut down.

Facebook and Friendster

Friendster was one of the original social networking sites. Founded by Jonathan Abrams and launched in 2002, Friendster grew rapidly, securing over three million users within the first few months of going live. However, ultimately Friendster was overtaken by MySpace in 2004 and then MySpace was similarly overtaken by Facebook. Unlike the two companies that preceded it, Facebook at this point appears to have created a service with significant staying power: The company today is valued at more than $270 billion. Facebook initially limited the website's membership to Harvard students, later expanding it to colleges in the Boston area, the Ivy League, and Stanford University before eventually opening it to all universities, high-school students, and finally to anyone who is at least 13 years old. With almost 1.5 billion users in 2015, Facebook remains the world's most popular social network.

LinkedIn and Spoke

LinkedIn is a business/professional-oriented social networking service launched on May 5, 2003. It was founded by Reid Hoffman, formerly of PayPal, and four co-founders. The site grew steadily in popularity. In 2015 it had over 365 million users in more than 200 countries. Spoke, a site launched at about the same time, was also designed to offer an online solution for professional networking as well as a business directory. Although Spoke is still in operation today, Internet audience measurement firm Quantcast estimates it is getting less than 200,000 visitors a month.

Hotmail and Juno

Although hard to remember today, at one point, most individuals got their personal email address through their Internet service provider, such as America Online. Hotmail sought to change this by providing free web-based email. Hotmail service was founded by Sabeer Bhatia and Jack Smith, and was one of the first webmail services on the Internet. It was launched on July 4, 1996, and by December 1997 had over 8.5 million subscribers—which was quite a large number back when most people were still using dial-up. Hotmail was acquired by Microsoft for $400 million on New Year's Eve 1997.

One of the company's early competitors was Juno, founded in 1996 by Charles Ardai, Brian Marsh, and Clifford Tse with significant venture capital investment and a marketing budget of $20 million. Juno would go public in May 1999 and ultimately merge with NetZero after two years of lawsuits between the two.

Cvent and StarCite

Cvent and StarCite both sought to make event/meeting planning easier by creating a software-as-a-service (SaaS) that provided meetings/event management technology. Cvent was founded in September 1999 and after enduring a very tumultuous few years, surviving first the dot-com bubble burst and then the corporate travel restrictions imposed after September 11, it has gone on to become the leading name in meeting/event management software and today is a publicly traded company with over a $1 billion valuation. Meanwhile its competitor StarCite failed to achieve the same success and was eventually purchased by Active Networks for $51.8 million.

McDonald's and White Castle

McDonald's and White Castle are two famous fast-food hamburger chains. While McDonald's is now larger, White Castle, founded in Wichita, Kansas, in 1921, is generally credited as the inventor of the category. While still in business today, it has about 345 restaurants in operation nationwide. On the other hand, McDonald's—started a few decades later—has gone on to be the world's largest fast-food chain, serving around 68 million customers daily in 119 countries across 35,000 outlets, with a market cap of $96 billion.

Google

Although it started exclusively as an Internet search engine, based on research by Larry Page and Sergey Brin while they were PhD students at Stanford University, Google has grown to offer numerous other products. While it was tempting to compare Google to one of the other early search engines, I ultimately decided it wasn't a fair comparison. By the time Google entered the market, search was undervalued relative to other initiatives. In fact, until February 2004 Google actually powered the search on Yahoo's home page.[8]

PayPal

PayPal was originally a novel encryption technology and then moved to focus on making it easy for people to pay each other digitally. While this focus began on transfers via PalmPilots, PayPal ultimately achieved scale by making it easy to transfer money over email. The service grew very rapidly: It went public in 2002 and soon after was purchased by eBay for $1.3 billion. Only recently (July 2015) PayPal was spun back out of eBay and went public at a $46.5 billion valuation.

The team members who took part in founding and growing PayPal have gone on to become some of Silicon Valley's most successful entrepreneurs, earning the group the moniker the "PayPal Mafia."

The two companies that would have been most interesting to contrast with PayPal actually merged to form PayPal. The company began when Confinity, founded by Max Levchin, Peter Thiel, Luke Nosek, and Ken Howery, merged with Elon Musk's X.com in 2000.

Twitter

Twitter is an online social networking site that allows registered users to send and read short 140-character messages called "tweets." Twitter was created in March 2006 as a spin-off of the company Odeo (a service that was focused on podcasting but never achieved tremendous growth). Today Twitter has more than 500 million users and is a publicly traded company with a market cap over $21 billion.

Dropbox

Dropbox is a file-sharing service. It syncs your work across all your devices. Your digital files are backed up and you can even return to older versions or restore deleted files. The company was founded in 2007 by MIT students Drew Houston and Arash Ferdowsi. Dropbox now has over 400 million users and a valuation of over $10 billion.

A common question about our research is why we didn't compare Dropbox with Box. We did investigate this potential early on, but came to believe that while the products were similar their markets at the beginning were different enough that it made comparing them difficult. Dropbox was very successful at getting individual consumers to adopt its solution and only later moved into the enterprise market. Box focused on enterprise customers much earlier. While I believe they are increasingly competitive today, the early markets and techniques were different enough that both were able to achieve plenty of growth and are now multibillion-dollar companies.

Airbnb

Airbnb is a website that provides a marketplace for people to rent out their spare rooms or their homes. Airbnb is now valued at more than $25 billion and has over one million listings in 190 countries. With continued strong growth Airbnb looks poised to continue its disruption of the travel lodging industry.

Uber

Uber, founded in 2009 by Travis Kalanick and Garrett Camp, solved a real problem of ineffective taxi service in most cities. The company developed a smartphone app that transparently connected riders with black car operators. Today Uber has expanded that service beyond black cars to drivers of other vehicles, including individuals who are using their own cars (the basic idea is similar to Airbnb). This simple solution has made the company massively popular and earned it a valuation of $50 billion.

As with our decision not to compare Box and Dropbox, a lot of people I've discussed this research with have asked why I didn't compare Lyft and Uber. I believe these companies, like Box and Dropbox, are quite competitive today but early on Uber and Lyft took very different approaches, with Lyft focusing on making everyone a driver while Uber partnered with black car operators.

WHAT DID WE FIND?

With those overviews of our chosen companies complete, let's come back to our findings. As we looked across the case studies of our chosen companies, we ended up segmenting our findings into three categories:

First, we developed a set of four prerequisites that, while insufficient on their own to allow a company to ultimately scale up, we believe are essential to have in place right out of the gate:

Prerequisite 1—Founder's Core Vision: It's difficult to overstate the importance of founders in a company's ultimate success. In addition to leadership, it's important that the problem the entrepreneurs set out to solve is one they are passionate about and prepared to address.

Prerequisite 2—Scalable Idea: You can't scale a startup that serves a market of only a few people or organizations.

Prerequisite 3—Solves a Real Problem: The large market (Prerequisite 2) must actually get value from the solution that you have developed.

Prerequisite 4—An Excellent First Interaction: This is the final of the four prerequisites because you can deal with it last. As you start to focus on scaling, you must make sure the world's first interaction with your product is not just good, but excellent.

We will elaborate on each of these prerequisites in chapters 2 through 5.

Once you have satisfied each of the four preceding prerequisites, the next step is to think through what you can do to accelerate your growth. We identified four best practices, or catalysts, entrepreneurs should consider as they try to accelerate growth. Each of these techniques attempts to answer the question: **How can I increase awareness among those people who would find my solution valuable?** The idea is not that every innovation will leverage all of these catalysts, but that just one or more of these catalysts can dramatically accelerate your growth.

Catalyst 1—Double Trigger Events: In the evolution of many of our chosen startups, there were events not governed by the company which accelerated company growth by increasing awareness of its product. People often think of these events later as the company's "launch" event, even though the company usually released the product publicly months before.

Catalyst 2—Drafting off of Platforms: In other cases the catalyst is not an event in time, but is instead a large, existing platform of engaged individuals who are looking proactively for your solution to augment their experience on a current platform.

Catalyst 3—Optimizing Algorithms: Over the last decade, as software (search engines, app stores, and mobile recommenda- tion apps) became a more significant way to discover products and services, an effective way to increase awareness has become optimizing the rules those systems use to recommend solutions so your startup is at the top of the list.

Catalyst 4—Viral Growth: The last way to dramatically increase the number of potential customers who are aware of your product or service is to get your existing customers to tell their colleagues and friends. While using existing customers as a referral service predates the Internet, current tools and technologies make this channel much easier to optimize.

We will elaborate on each of these catalysts in chapters 6 through 9. Finally, the last step is to focus on making sure you have the foundations for long-term sustained success. After studying our chosen companies, the team and I concluded there were five elements that served as the foundation for sustained growth.

Foundational Element 1—Be Data Informed, Not Data Driven: How to handle data is a crucial question most organizations are asking themselves today. It's easy either to become too reliant on data for answers, or conversely, to ignore data and just rely on your creative instinct and vision. The chosen companies struck a bal- ance by being data informed, but not data driven.

Foundational Element 2—Finance Growth Appropriately: While it has become less and less expensive to test an idea, it is still very expensive, in most cases, to scale a startup. Specifically, it is very difficult to support explosive growth using only the cash provided by organic operations. Therefore, your company needs to determine the right financing strategy if it is to thrive while scaling.

Foundational Element 3—Recruit a High-Performing Team: As you scale, it becomes important that your organization creates a culture to attract and retain high-performing individuals who complement the team and accelerate growth. While this may seem obvious, as no one sets out to recruit a low-performing team, we tried to spend time unpacking how, exactly, the companies we chose succeeded in recruiting these high-performers.

Foundational Element 4—Maintain Discipline: If high-performing teams are the most obvious element, this was the least obvious. I expected that the companies that scaled would have a variety of initiatives going on. But instead, as we looked at our chosen companies, it became clear that they were ruthlessly disciplined, prioritizing and focusing only on the activities most important to their strategy.

Foundational Element 5—Maximize the Value of Your Network: Finally, as the last of our five foundational elements, we talk about strategies to maximize the value of the networks being developed. There may be no term more misused than "network effects," but when a company really starts to scale, they do end up creating actual network effects.

We will elaborate on these foundational elements for long-term growth in chapters 10 through 14.

UNVALIDATED HYPOTHESES

As the team and I looked at our chosen companies, we explored a number of hypotheses that we were not able to validate. Before we jump into the rest of this book and look at our findings, I thought it would be helpful to point out the two hypotheses we held at the start of this exploration that we could not validate with our case studies.

Figure 1.1 Elements for Sustained Long-Term Growth

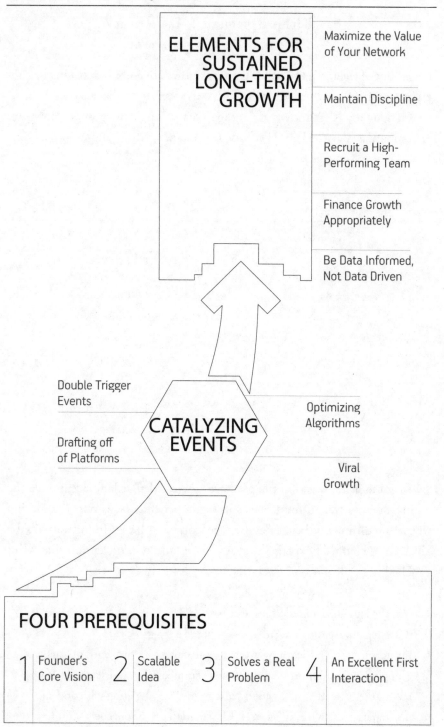

Unvalidated Hypothesis 1: The company that "moves first" is the winner

In fact, out of the ten pairs of companies studied, in eight instances, the successful company was started later. This was interesting, because we hear so much about the "first mover advantage" that it's become gospel. However, for companies like YouTube, Facebook, LinkedIn, Mint, and even McDonald's, the opposite was true.

Table 1.3 First to Market

FIRST MOVER	SECOND MOVER
Tumblr	Mint
Tesla	Automattic
	YouTube
	Facebook
	LinkedIn
	Hotmail
	Cvent
	McDonald's

In some of these cases, people have suggested that launching after the original startup was in market was in fact a benefit. In his post diagnosing why Mint ultimately beat Wesabe, the company he co-founded, Wesabe CEO Marc Hedlund explains that it's a common misconception that Mint launched first. He goes on to clarify:

> Wesabe launched about 10 months before Mint. More the shame that we didn't capitalize on that early lead. There's a lot to be said for not rushing to market, and learning from the mistakes the first entrants make. Shipping a "minimum viable product" immediately and learning from the market directly makes good sense to me, but engaging with and supporting users is anything but free. Observation can be cheaper. Mint (and

some others) did well by seeing where we screwed up, and waiting to launch until they had a better approach.[9]

It's also worth pointing out that in one of the two cases in which the company that started first ultimately succeeded—Tesla—its product, premium electric vehicles, already existed. In fact, as we'll describe more in Chapter 2, there was a startup, AC Propulsion, that created the "tzero," which largely served as the inspiration for the Tesla.

Unvalidated Hypothesis 2: The company that raises the largest first round of funding wins

Another common belief, like the first mover advantage, is that the startup that raises the most money early in its development wins the market. Speaking as a venture capitalist (VC), it would be wonderful if the data backed this up. It would imply that success is as simple as putting more capital to work in one company than in any of its competitors. As we'll discuss in the chapter on financing strategies (Chapter 11), you do need significant growth capital in most situations. However, as the table below shows, in most of the paired companies we looked at, both raised approximately the same amount of venture capital in their early financing rounds.[10]

I should mention, of course, that neither McDonald's nor White Castle received venture capital. However, I will later argue that McDonald's use of

Table 1.4 First Financing

LARGER	ABOUT THE SAME	SMALLER
Automattic	Tumblr	Mint
Cvent	YouTube	Hotmail
	Facebook	
	LinkedIn	
	McDonald's	

real estate and franchising to finance its growth was a crucial ingredient for its success—and one that White Castle avoided. Either way, in the earliest days both companies were on equal footing, so the point stands.

WHY IS HOW TO SCALE SUCH AN IMPORTANT QUESTION?

Now that you know where we are heading, and what we didn't validate, let's return to why this question of *how to scale your startup* is so profound. In my current role as a VC, I invest across a set of portfolio companies. At the time of each investment, I project that each one will deliver asymmetric returns relative to the amount of capital I risk investing in the company.

Put another way, I can lose up to the amount of money I invested in a startup, but forecast that investment returning more than ten times if the company ultimately goes on to be successful. This is important, because the investors that I raise money from expect me to return about three times as much capital back to them at the end of my fund's life (typically eight to ten years).

The fatality rate of startups at the early stage in which I invest is high—about one-third of the startups fail completely. Another third return some very small amount of the capital invested. This means that the last third drive most of the returns.

Those returns need to be roughly three times the total capital I was originally given to invest, alongside my own personal capital. Therefore, that last third need to return many multiples of the capital invested for the math to work. They're essentially paying for the failures as well as themselves.

Beyond classifying investments into those three broad buckets, great early stage venture portfolios typically follow an exponential return curve. Often, the best investment in the fund returns as much as the rest of the investments do in aggregate. Similarly, the second-best investment's returns are about the same as the returns of the third through the rest of the portfolio, and so on. This is different from a mutual fund, for example, or most other investment vehicles, in which the risk of each investment is lower, and therefore the expected returns can be lower, while it's still a worthwhile investment.

If you ever took a college finance course, you were probably taught about the correlation between risk and reward in any given investment. Early stage investing is extremely risky, so it requires high returns to successfully work across a portfolio.

Before I became a VC, I was an entrepreneur for a dozen years working on three different startups. From that perspective, this *Science of Growth* material is even more important. The most valuable resource any of us has is our time. Once a startup has that magical moment in which its product solves a real problem for a replicable and significant group of customers, it is in the entrepreneur's best interest to make sure the company scales to achieve the financial returns and, more important, the impact the entrepreneur dreamed of when starting out. While it's harder to quantify than a dollar invested and ten-plus dollars returned, I believe that a firm understanding of the principles discussed here gives an entrepreneur the greatest chance of asymmetric returns on the investment of their time.

WHY IS SCALING STARTUPS SO IMPORTANT TO ECONOMIC DEVELOPMENT?

Many regions across the world are trying to become "the next Silicon Valley." I think this is a terrible way to explain a region's startup community goals and I often encourage civic and economic development leaders to instead focus on becoming the best version of *their* city they can be. That said, encouraging high-growth entrepreneurship is critical for a region's long-term health; it has been clearly demonstrated in research led by the Kauffman Foundation that new job growth is driven not by large corporations but by high-growth startups.[11] Put another way, I'd argue the best versions of most cities include some high-growth startup ecosystem.

To encourage entrepreneurship, many cities have created regionally focused accelerators. By accelerator, I'm specifically referring to an early stage investment model in which the startup joins up with a number of other startups at the same time (a cohort of startups) and receives financial support, office space, and mentorship that concludes with a presentation—typically called the "demo day"—to a group of investors and influencers. The first of these, to my knowledge, was Y Combinator, an accelerator started in 2005 by Paul Graham. It helped launch Dropbox and Airbnb, among others.

I was personally involved in advising the creation of Pittsburgh's first accelerator—AlphaLab—in 2008; it's consistently ranked as one of the country's top 20 accelerators to this day.[12] In the last few years, hundreds of accelerators have been created across the world, many of them sponsored by economic development organizations and local leaders. But what these leaders and organizations often fail to realize is that the real challenge is not to get a lot of startups created, but to make sure the companies that are successful ultimately go on to be *really*, transformatively, high-growth. It's these successful startups that will ultimately drive significant job growth and financial returns.

Coming back to Y Combinator, the fact that they were involved in helping launch companies like Dropbox and Airbnb is what led so many other accelerators to copy their model and not dozens of other early startups that didn't work out. It's also the success of those two companies that has driven most of Y Combinator's financial performance. On the Y Combinator website, they explain that they have invested in over 800 companies, which have a combined valuation of over $30 billion. This would seem to imply an average valuation of greater than $37.5 million per company. However, the returns are not spread out equally. Instead, two of these companies (Airbnb and Dropbox) together account for $35 billion between them.

WHO IS THIS BOOK FOR?

If growth is a critical metric for your organization, this book is for you! It will provide you a set of best practices for doing your job better.

Our research has focused on startups, and is especially relevant for entrepreneurs who are entering the scaling phase. However, in my interactions with executives at larger companies, I've come to appreciate that many of these principles are also applicable to large companies looking to grow by entering new markets. These leaders seek to achieve scale on their innovative projects, and the best practices that follow should help them do that.

I've also had the opportunity to test some of the best practices with large industrial organizations, to see how relevant they feel outside of business-to-consumer environments. In my conversations with these B2B executives, the principles we've identified have closely matched the approaches used in the executives' most successful new product introductions and ventures, and are missing from their less successful projects.

Finally, I've also met with many nonprofit groups, from political organizations to churches and relief groups, all trying to figure out how to scale their communities. Many of the best practices discussed here have proven to be applicable to those organizations as well.

One thing I'm often asked when describing this research and now book is, Is it simply about how to become a "growth hacker"?

If you aren't familiar with the term "growth hacker," it was a job title coined by Sean Ellis, Hiten Shah, and Patrick Vlaskovits in 2010 to describe a new approach to marketing focused on an iterative and data-driven method to scaling customers once a business achieves product-market fit. There has been a lot written on the rise of growth hackers within startups. The concept is great and highlights the increased emphasis on taking a more analytic approach to marketing.

However, in my experience, it has become common for entrepreneurs to explain that once they achieve product-market fit (and sometimes even before that), they'll "just hire one of these magical growth hackers" and then, by implication, just sit back and watch their business scale. This book will show you that there is an entire science to growth, so in some ways many of these techniques may indeed help growth hackers. But as we explored and analyzed the cases, I became convinced that for a company to scale, the entire company needs to be committed to that goal of growth and not simply delegate it to one person or team.

Whether you are a CEO at a venture-backed startup trying to achieve scale to IPO your startup or a pastor at a local church trying to reach a larger percentage of your local community, I hope the best practices shared in this book will help you and your team achieve your vision and, as Steve Jobs famously said, "dent the universe."

SECTION I

PREREQUISITES FOR SCALING

WHEN LAUNCHING A STARTUP, IT'S TEMPTING TO JUMP IMMEDIATELY TO the issues covered in the second and third sections of this book. After all, you already know your product is perfect and the market is ready for it. However, I want to pause here and offer a word of caution.

In 2010 and 2011, a group of researchers, mostly out of the University of California, Berkeley and Stanford University, gathered and analyzed longitudinal data on over 3,200 startups, in an effort ambitiously named "The Startup Genome Project." They broke the development of a startup into six distinct phases and then evaluated each startup using machine-learning algorithms to assess if the startups included in their study kept product, team, financial, and business-model advancement consistent with the feedback from their customers. Here are a few key findings from a report they issued in 2011, focused specifically on their findings around premature scaling:

> 74% of high growth internet startups fail due to premature scaling . . . no startup that scaled prematurely passed the 100,000 user mark.
> 93% of startups that scale prematurely never break the $100k revenue per month threshold.[1]

The outside pressure to skip over the prerequisites described in the next four chapters is real. I have felt it as an entrepreneur and truth be told I've even given into it at times. Today as a VC, I try very hard to be balanced and to be a great partner for the entrepreneurs that I work with, but I'm sure I have inadvertently pressured some of them to move on to scaling prematurely—the desire to grow quickly is simply human nature and entrepreneurs are typically not very patient people.

We all want to move on to the challenges of winning the market and changing the world. No one starts or invests in a startup with the hope that it will stay focused on these first few prerequisites. However, as "The Startup Genome" research has quantified, trying to grow quickly without first putting the right foundation in place will ultimately lead to frustration and failure.

2

FOUNDER'S CORE VISION

"Everyone has a great plan until they get punched in the mouth."

—Mike Tyson

FOUNDERS START THEIR ENTREPRENEURIAL ADVENTURE WITH LITTLE MORE than core insights that serve as the foundation of their powerful vision. The successful ones will invest years of their lives into making this vision a reality. When you later read an article profiling the success of these founders, their vision may seem obvious, and the progress linear. Yet, neither is true for a long, tumultuous period.

Later in this book we will talk about the importance of high-performance teams (Chapter 12) as you scale up for growth, but the foundation of a startup is based on the founding team's vision of how to solve a given problem. Without a strong foundation, no matter how compelling the product or market, the startup will not succeed.

This founding team sets the startup's initial direction and generates momentum when resistance is at its highest. As discussed in the first chapter, entrepreneurs create the world the way it ought to be and a founder is often the first to communicate the vision of that world. Unfortunately, the real world often takes time to catch up.

Even if you've never been part of a startup, you are probably able to intuitively understand the role that a founder's vision and passion play. Still, we tend to underestimate its importance.

Experiments conducted at the turn of this century at Dow Chemical actually went so far as to identify the ideal personality profile for individuals leading a new business initiative in its early stages.

The company studied 267 different new product initiatives within its organization. These initiatives were spread across ten years and led by 69 different analysts. This analysis led Dow to develop an ideal personality profile for applying Dow's staged-gate development. When applied to future projects, this insight "led to increase in NBP [New Business Development] speed and effectiveness of more than 900 percent, by achieving near-perfection in commercialization rates."[1]

While Dow analysts leading new business development are not the same as founders, the 900 percent improvement certainly provides some context for how important a great founder is to a startup's success. So let's start our review of these prerequisites by looking at the early founders of the companies we studied and how their personality, insights, and passion matched up so well to the ambitious visions they set out to pursue.

TESLA

Martin Eberhard, the co-founder and first CEO of Tesla, had already started and sold multiple startups before turning his attention to electric vehicles. In fact, it was his personal interest in buying a sports car that inspired him to found the company. He wanted to buy a sports car, but given the geopolitical environment, was reluctant to buy a car that got less than twenty miles per gallon—even if it could go from 0 to 60 incredibly quickly.

So he investigated different energy options for cars. He calculated how much energy is required from natural resources to make a car go a mile. He looked at everything from hydrogen fuel cells, to various kinds of gasoline and diesel, to natural gas, to several types of batteries. Looking back, he remembers: "The results were quite startling . . . Hydrogen fuel cells are terrible. Their energy efficiency is no better than gas. Electric cars were head and shoulders above everything else, even if you made the electricity out of coal."[2]

At that time, General Motors was experimenting with its own electrical vehicle, the EV1. This was an electric car that was only available for lease as a controlled experiment from the GM advanced technology group. In fact, the vehicles were only produced in response to a California mandate that the major automakers start producing and selling zero-emission cars if they wanted to continue selling any cars in the state.

The *New York Times* and others in the media would later argue that GM never gave the EV1 a real shot.[3] Whether a fair criticism or not, GM did eventually pull the leases, and never allowed customers to purchase the EV1. GM held firm even after some former lease owners sent in checks and had documents drawn up releasing GM of all liability. A few dedicated fans even staged a round-the-clock protest for months trying to keep the cars from being destroyed.[4]

General Motors' initial official response to this reaction was to state that while there was a passionate market for an electric vehicle, it was far too limited to support a viable business.[5] In hindsight, GM readily acknowledges it shouldn't have pulled the plug on the EV1.[6] However, at the time of Tesla's founding, the fledgling company's vision was a future of electric vehicles far less limited than GM predicted.

This faith wasn't based on idealism alone. Tesla's founders knew they could create high-performing electric vehicles. They already had experience with boutique electric car manufacturer AC Propulsion and its handmade sample sports car, the "tzero." Martin referenced this experience in the original Tesla business plan.

The first time I drove the AC Propulsion tzero, I was immediately struck by the way the power didn't fade as the car accelerated—it felt like a race car in first gear, but a first gear that just kept going and going, all the way to 100 mph.

The second revelation was how quickly I came just to expect the power or engine braking to be there when I wanted it—not even to think about downshifting. The power control had become as simple and instinctive as basic steering control.

Thirdly, at the end of the run, I was amazed at how smooth, precise and easy the speed control was at parking speeds. After all, I'm still in the same gear I was just using to do 100 mph, and there's not even a clutch! How can this be?[7]

In fact, at one point, Eberhard invested in and thought about joining the AC Propulsion team.[8] Even after he decided that joining the team wouldn't work, under Martin's leadership Tesla tried to license some of the technology, and it informed their initial vision.[9]

It was also more than a financial motivation that made co-founder Elon Musk so committed to building Tesla. When asked in an interview what advice he'd give someone starting a car company, he responded:

> It's an extremely capital-intensive industry. It should certainly not be anyone's choice if they are trying to get the highest return on investment.
>
> So my first advice would be, unless they have some compelling non-monetary reason to create a car company, as I did, [then] this is not a good use of their capital . . .
>
> My goal is to accelerate the advent of the electric car by whatever means necessary. And if we simply tried to sell electric powertrain technology to the car companies we would have had no success. We need to show by example.[10]

This was clearly very important to him. In a different interview, Musk talked about being very excited at first when the largest car company (GM) created the EV1, and he called the decision to cancel it "tone deaf." Musk said the GM experience demonstrated that "there really needs to be a new car company that comes in and shows that it can be done"—he later defined "it" as creating a "good looking, high performance, long range" electric vehicle that people would willingly buy.[11]

LINKEDIN

Reid Hoffman, years after founding LinkedIn, would explain on his personal blog:

> It's said that when architects walk through an office, they see ceiling ornamentation, light sources, building acoustics. When psychologists walk through an office, they see unresolved father issues and avoidant

personality disorders. When I walk through an office, I see networks. I know that makes me sound like the kid from *The Sixth Sense*. But I don't see dead people. I see networks.

When you truly see networks, it changes the way you plan and strategize. You move differently.[12]

While the founders had conviction about the professional network's value, they weren't certain everyone else would get it at first. LinkedIn co-founder Konstantin Guericke later explained that the team contemplated, early on, the possibility that no one else would see the value of this professional network. Hoffman was so passionate about the utility for himself that he would single-handedly pay to keep the service minimally operational if only for his own use.[13] Years later, of course, millions of individuals pay for a LinkedIn premium account to advance their own careers.

Even after 900,000 members had signed up for the professional network, LinkedIn still felt compelled to overemphasize the potential value of the company in its Series B pitch. Years later, after LinkedIn went public, Hoffman would publish the slide deck used to raise that Series B financing and add his commentary. In a post reviewing the deck, he explained:

> We argued that the way professional people search was done at the time ("1.0") was inadequate. To make this argument, we listed three important professional business problems (finding service providers, finding job candidates, and reaching professionals) that were time-consuming and difficult to accomplish with existing technologies . . .
>
> So, how do you create a platform where talented professionals can participate, be found, and be contactable? Our answer: a network.[14]

And he went on to elaborate:

> Most technology revolutions are founded on one or two simple concepts. Our simple concept was: "The network provides the platform for a new kind of people search, which can be a platform to many other businesses."

Today millions of LinkedIn members have experienced the value of a professional network. Yet at the time, as with Tesla's vision of electric vehicles, it took conviction to create it.

FACEBOOK

Mark Zuckerberg's intuition about the power and value of people using technology to connect with each other is legendary. At a speech in San Francisco in 2008, Zuckerberg reportedly said: "I would expect that next year, people will share twice as much information as they share this year, and next year, they will be sharing twice as much as they did the year before . . ."[15]

The *New York Times,* covering the speech, coined the phrase "Zuckerberg's Law" to describe this statement (comparing it to the famous Moore's Law from 1965, which predicted with amazing accuracy that microprocessors would double in efficiency every year).

The trend Zuckerberg described has continued, and while the prediction at the time seemed extreme, it was in fact prescient. Three years later, at a Facebook announcement in 2011, Zuckerberg went to great pains to try to quantify the impact of exponential growth and show how difficult it is for humans to grasp the rate at which things grow.[16]

While the "Zuckerberg Law" is just one example, it is clear Zuckerberg has a deep understanding of how individuals interact with technology. This understanding has driven the vision and direction of the company. His control over the trajectory was established on day one, and reinforced regularly as the company grew.

Another example of this vision occurred early in Facebook's development, at a point when many other first-time founders might have been intimidated and adjusted their plans based on the experience of other senior leaders. When an early Facebook executive, Doug Hirsch, tried to orchestrate the sale of Facebook to Yahoo, Zuckerberg held his ground and fired Hirsch. Noah Kagan, who began work at Facebook as employee number 30 on the day his expected boss Hirsch received the boot, explained Zuckerberg's reasoning in his 2014 book, *How I Lost 170 Million Dollars:*

Whenever asked, he [Zuckerberg] publicly stated, a line he firmly believed, "Facebook is being built for long-term success. Just like Google." That [Doug Hirsch] firing was a very clear lesson that it was Mark's company and he got to do what he wanted to do with it. He fired Doug immediately when he found Doug trying to get the deal to go through behind his back.[17]

While it would be easy to interpret this as a monarchy controlled by the founder, Zuckerberg was very quick to delegate authority in key areas outside his expertise to Sheryl Sandberg, once he recruited her to join the team.

Sandberg, who had spent time in Washington and worked at Google after graduating from Harvard, joined the team and immediately started focusing on how to scale up the organization—including trying to devise a strategy that would enable the site to make money. Zuckerberg trusted her efforts in this completely. It was, in part, to reinforce her authority that Zuckerberg actually spent a month out of the office traveling around the world, while Sandberg convened meetings to discuss how to achieve these goals, ultimately landing on targeted advertising after also considering charging members of Facebook for its use.[18]

WHO "COUNTS" AS A FOUNDER?

Sheryl Sandberg joining Mark Zuckerberg at Facebook illustrates an important point: Founders often augment their team with people who may not technically have been on the team on day one, but still operate like founders.

This leads to an important question: Who do you consider a founder? Legally, there is an easy definition for this question: Founders are those individuals who own founder's stock. In reality, it's often much more complicated. Employees who join the company early often have significant influence over the product and business direction, such that they end up helping to shape the company: Those individuals may later be called co-founders.

No one from our study may be a better example of this than McDonald's Ray Kroc, who was not involved in the original business started by brothers Richard and Maurice McDonald. However, it was Kroc's vision and perseverance that led to the company's success.

Kroc was also joined for ten years by Harry Sonneborn, a vice president at Tastee-Freez, who, after observing one of the early McDonald's restaurants, quit his job and called Kroc to explain: "I can tell just by watching it [a McDonald's store] from across the street that you've got a winner there, Mr. Kroc and I'd like to be part of your organization."[19] After their first meeting, Kroc told Sonneborn that he felt the former Tastee-Freez VP would be incredibly helpful, but wasn't sure how he could afford him. Sonneborn said he'd come back with the lowest possible salary he could afford to accept. Kroc described what followed:

> In a few days, Harry called back and said he could come to work for $100 a week take-home pay. It was an offer I couldn't refuse. Good thing for McDonald's that I didn't, because the company could never have grown as it did without the unique vision of Harry Sonneborn.[20]

We'll go into more details in Chapter 11, but in addition to being responsible for legal and financial details, it was Sonneborn who came up with the real estate investment strategy that ultimately fueled McDonald's amazing growth.

Another interesting example of a late co-founder comes from Automattic. Founder Matt Mullenweg added Toni Schneider as the CEO for roughly eight years during a critical phase of the company's development. Schneider came from Yahoo, to which he had recently sold a company (Oddpost) that coupled early innovation in web-based email with an innovative approach to news aggregation. While the price of the acquisition was never disclosed, speculation in the media was roughly $30 million. Oddpost only raised one round of financing before the acquisition, so this was likely a fine outcome for investors and early employees.[21]

At the time Schneider joined the firm, Automattic was a four-person company and only a few months old. Mullenweg was in his early twenties and had a bold vision for the future of publishing; he found in Schneider a partner who would help him grow Automattic into a billion-dollar company with over 230 employees and with 20 percent of Internet websites built on the platform. Schneider led the company until a few days after Mullenweg's thirtieth birthday, when they "switched roles" and Mullenweg took over as CEO.[22]

Google did something very similar, with Eric Schmidt running the company as CEO for a decade before Larry Page returned to the CEO seat.

However, no one has better explained the point that founders can be a broader group than simply the day-one employees than Jack Dorsey. Jack was one of the founders of Twitter, a company that went through more leadership changes than most high-growth startups. At a technology conference in San Francisco, Jack discussed the role of a founder:

> A lot of people consider Ev, Biz and myself to be the founders of the company. But that ignores the reality, companies exist and evolve over time and in fact they have multiple founding moments. So I consider Dick Costolo, our CEO, a Founder. He's had such a dramatic impact on the company, the culture, what we are doing that he's questioned everything we started with and made it better . . . An idea that can change the course of the company can come from anywhere. A founder is not a job. It's a role. It's an attitude. It's something that can happen again and again.[23]

BEYOND VISION, WHAT'S A FOUNDER'S ROLE?

At the start, founders usually focus on two critical tasks: acquiring customers, and delighting those customers with their solution. I find this is often one of the most challenging things for business school students to understand, given their work experience at large corporations. When teaching graduate courses in entrepreneurship as part of an MBA program, I will ask students, "What role do you plan to contribute to a founding team?" They answer things like human resources, strategy, or finance. While clearly all of these are important functions at the average Fortune 500 company, they are not, unfortunately, the critical ingredients for getting a startup off the ground.

In a startup, those functions usually develop during the process of executing against sales and delivery goals. Take, for example, corporate culture. No one would argue that a strong and healthy culture is not important. As John Kotter and James Heskett first quantified in 1992,[24] there is a strong correlation between financial performance and a vibrant, healthy corporate culture.

However, in most startups, the founders and early employees create a strong and healthy culture just by doing their jobs, and making the stories from those early days part of their corporate psyche. They need no specific initiative to "create" the desired culture.

For example, in our study we found that Cvent retains to this day the practice of executives sharing hotel rooms when they travel. This maps back to early in the company's development when the founders established that cultural norm, and it still has symbolic, if not financial, value.

Another important point: A sole founder rarely wears two hats—the founder focuses either on acquiring new customers or delighting them with solutions, not both. I often tell my students, if they are going to contribute to the sales function in a startup, the first sale they need to make is to a technical co-founder who will "buy" with the most valuable resource he or she has—time. Beyond simply having someone to share responsibilities with, you will have someone who is equally committed to the vision of the startup with whom you can work through strategic issues.

PERSEVERANCE

In addition to executing early sales and delivery functions, founders also provide the necessary tenacity to persevere in challenging moments. The founder of Carnegie Mellon University's Tepper (MBA) Entrepreneurship Program, Jack Thorne, used to define the practice to students as follows: "Entrepreneurship is insane perseverance in the face of constant rejection."

Almost every startup in our study went through a period of disillusionment in which failure seemed inevitable. In these situations, the founders' commitment to success as the only option was critical to the company's surviving and ultimately thriving.

No story may illustrate this point better than that of Elon Musk at Tesla. By the time Musk got involved in Tesla, he had already co-founded and sold two companies—the first, Zip2, an early mapping service acquired by Compaq for $307 million, from which he earned $22 million; and the second, PayPal, which made almost ten times as much for Musk when it was sold to eBay for $1.5 billion.

Unfortunately, after getting involved in Tesla as an early and very involved investor he took on a similar role in a few other companies (SpaceX and Solar City). He had invested all of his capital into getting those businesses going. In fact, right before Christmas in 2008 Musk only had $3 million of liquidity when he found out that Tesla was not going to make payroll. Looking back on that moment, in an interview with *Men's Journal* in 2011, he described the choice as: "Either I went all in, or Tesla dies . . . I didn't want to look back and say there was something more I could have done and didn't." So, according to the article, "he wrote the check [to cover payroll] and went home wondering how he would pay the next month's rent."[25]

There is an element of insane perseverance that is just built into the DNA of great founders. Ray Kroc, in his autobiography, explains how even from a young age he'd dream something up, then set out to work hard and accomplish it:

> They called me Danny Dreamer a lot, even later when I was in high school and would come home all excited about some scheme I'd thought up. I never considered my dreams wasted energy; they were invariably linked to some form of action. When I dreamed about having a lemonade stand, for example, it wasn't long before I set up a lemonade stand. I worked hard at it, and I sold a lot of lemonade . . . I worked at something whenever possible. Work is the meat in the hamburger of life. There is an old saying that *all work and no play makes Jack a dull boy*. I never believed it because, for me, work was play.[26]

In the case of McDonald's, it really was Kroc's character trait of persistence that ultimately led to him even getting involved with McDonald's. There had been a number of visitors to the McDonald brothers' store in California long before Kroc. Some had even purchased franchises from the brothers directly. Others spent time watching the operation and then tried to replicate it on their own.

When Kroc met the brothers, he had already spent 25 years in the restaurant industry between selling paper cups and then later milkshake mixers across the country. In fact, it was Kroc's mixer business that prompted him to take the trip. His business as the exclusive marketer of Multi-Mixer (milkshake maker) had been extremely successful by selling to soda fountains in cities. Unfortunately, this success was short-lived. As families moved to the suburbs, the corner drugstore soda fountains declined and were replaced with suburban soft-serve ice cream chains like Dairy Queen and Tastee-Freez. These restaurants were not interested in Kroc's milkshake machines and so sales dried up. In 1953 he had to cut his staff dramatically, reducing his sales team from 11 to 2.

While Kroc was exploring and ultimately deciding against trying to find a different product, he got an order for his tenth mixer from the McDonalds. He also had orders from many of the people trying to copy the McDonald brothers' formula. These orders were the impetus for Kroc to go visit the McDonald's store in San Bernardino, California. Kroc realized that in many ways they were becoming his best salespeople.

Ultimately, he realized there was a much bigger future selling hamburgers than restaurant supplies—but the 25 years' experience persevering in the restaurant supply business would provide him a great foundation.[27]

That trait of perseverance, applied above to his distribution business, would also be needed as he built McDonald's. In the early years, cash flow was often a huge concern even as the company began to gain momentum. Often McDonald's had to call prospective franchisees and convince them to send in their $10,000 security deposits immediately to cover the next payroll. On one Friday afternoon, the finance department realized even that technique wouldn't cover the weekly payroll. To get additional time to solve the cash constraint, the company announced that, effective immediately, it was moving from a weekly to semimonthly pay period. That extra week provided just enough cover to keep the company afloat, and to this day McDonald's pays employees semimonthly.[28]

Another amazing story of founder perseverance comes from our case study on Cvent. Founder and CEO Reggie Aggarwal was a lawyer before leaving to start the company. After raising $17 million the company ramped up hiring and subsequently signed a lease for more office space before the markets changed dramatically (we'll spend more time on this story in Chapter 11 when discussing financing strategies). The dot-com Internet implosion, followed by the September 11 attacks, dramatically affected the corporate travel market.

Cvent had to cut their expenses by renegotiating the lease, reducing the amount of space used. The landlord required Aggarwal to personally guarantee the new lease. This would force him to declare personal bankruptcy if the business didn't work out. While bankruptcy is not a pleasant experience for anyone, it would have prevented corporate lawyer Aggarwal from ever being able to rejoin a top-tier law firm. After making sure all of his senior team was committed, Aggarwal signed the guarantee, dramatically reducing burn and creating part of the first phase of an expense reduction plan to get the business on a better path that would lead to a successful public offering at a valuation of over $1 billion 14 years later.[29]

PUTTING THIS INTO ACTION

Hopefully, this chapter has illustrated how and why strong founders committed to the vision of their startups are critical. If you consider strong founders and their visions as the first of four prerequisites, the question then becomes, how do you assess competency in this area? Unfortunately, while none of these prerequisites are *easy* to assess, this one is particularly challenging.

Starting with this chapter, and for the rest of this book, I'll end each chapter with a few questions you can ask yourself to put the chapter into action.

Question 1: What important truth do very few people agree with you on?

I first heard this question from Peter Thiel, who talks about its importance in his outstanding book *Zero to One*. Thiel was a founder of PayPal, and was later one of the first investors in Facebook. He's been a prescient contrarian in Silicon Valley for years, amassing a significant fortune. Today, he is a very successful VC and investor.

According to his book, this is a question he asks every entrepreneur he meets. As I've started to use this question myself, it's proven to be a powerful way to understand the convictions guiding the startup. It's these convictions that will help the entreprenuer's startup create the future, which leads to the second question.

Question 2: What will the world look like in three to five years if your startup is incredibly successful?

The phrasing of this question is really important. I don't want to know your revenue projections per se. In most cases, this is impossible to project and all you really know about those numbers is that they are wrong. The phrase is "what will the world look like." Great entrepreneurs create the world the way it ought to be. Typically, entrepreneurs' passion shines through when they answer this question. What broken thing in the world are you fixing? How will your product deliver value to your customers and, ultimately, their organization? If you're struggling with this question at the outset, reflect on the motivation driving you. You'll need it to persevere when you encounter challenges later in your startup.

3

SCALABLE IDEAS

"Markets that don't exist don't care how smart you are."

—Marc Andreessen[1]

WHAT IS THE WORST OUTCOME FOR A STARTUP? THE MOST OBVIOUS AN-
swer is going out of business. After walking with founders through the process of shutting their startup down, I certainly appreciate the sentiment.
It's emotionally difficult to shut down something into which you've invested time and resources. Even worse is having to let go employees who
have bought into your vision, and with whom you have worked side by side
through many sleepless nights trying to succeed.

However, I'd argue that there is an even more frustrating outcome for a
startup—building a product you're passionate about, with a small number
of people who care about your solution, only to realize there aren't enough
potential customers to justify the time and resources invested in the business. Especially when those core customers barely cover the cost of running
the business, leaving just enough salary for founders to scrape by but certainly not enough to cover the sunk opportunity cost of their time.

In the last few years, this outcome has become much more prevalent
in technology startups as fixed operating costs have decreased dramatically
with the advent of cloud computing and open-source software that can be
leveraged. While this is a wonderful trend overall, it does sometimes lead

to companies that are stuck in a purgatory: unwilling to shut the business down but also unsure how to drive growth to build meaningful levels.

Passion for your core vision is important, but it's not the only prerequisite to building a growing, viable business. This second prerequisite is making sure your idea is scalable enough to achieve the goals you set. For an idea to be scalable, it must have two critical ingredients:

1. Projected Economies of Scale
2. Large Total Addressable Market

One important note: I am going to avoid using absolute numbers in this chapter. I can't tell you how large a potential opportunity needs to be to be interesting to you. The important takeaway is that you need to evaluate this up front, instead of later being surprised by the small size of the market opportunity.

In the next two chapters, I'm going to focus less on distinctions between the paired companies we analyzed, because the startups in each pair were, by definition, targeting the same market with similar solutions. I believe both prerequisites are so important that I'm including them in this book, with relevant best practices highlighted from our chosen companies.

ECONOMIES OF SCALE

Economies of scale is an economic principle which states that unit costs decrease (often dramatically) as the organization's output increases.

Most ultimately scalable businesses will lose money on their first customer. Even when you ignore the fixed costs of creating the product and all related intellectual property, you often need to do non-scalable things in the early days to deliver on the value promised to your customers. However, assuming success and growth, an entrepreneur should project decreasing total unit costs as the business scales.

For an extreme example of this, let's contrast the difference between two businesses—Tesla and a doctor's office.

Tesla's business model includes inherent economies of scale. As Tesla produces more vehicles, it is able to spread out the cost of research and development, and as the company purchases larger batches of parts to be included in the cars, the vendors provide more competitive pricing. Therefore, the cost necessary to sell the first Tesla Roadster would be dramatically higher than the costs necessary to sell the most recent one.

On the other hand, if you think about your local primary care physician, the major costs are the salary of the physicians and support staff. These costs don't decrease dramatically as you move from one patient to a larger number of patients. While there are small cost savings associated with a few fixed costs such as real estate, in most cases the costs scale linearly with the services delivered. While doctors make a good living and certainly contribute greatly to society, they effectively trade their time for money. Whether you are a doctor, lawyer, or business consultant, when you trade time for money, time is a constrained resource (we all have 24 hours in a day) and so these are not scalable ideas.

All of the companies in our study benefited from economies of scale. It's easy to see how a company whose primary business is providing software benefits from scale. There are significant fixed costs involved in designing and developing the software, but incremental customers have a minimal cost.

The company for which the advantage of scale may be least obvious is McDonald's, but the firm did invest real capital into product development. In 1957, franchise owners led by Louis Martino convinced Kroc to open a laboratory to study and standardize the process of creating McDonald's foods. Martino, who had left an electrical engineering job at Motorola to open a McDonald's franchise with his wife, had already been doing experiments in the basement of his franchise. Martino would investigate everything from the impact of the temperature of the frying vats when dropping in cold potatoes, to the starch vs sugar content of ideal potatoes for french fries. The investments were significant for an organization that still had a net worth of less than $100,000 and was struggling with cash flow. Gerry Newman, chief accounting officer of McDonald's at the time, estimated that the company spent over $3 million in the first decade on R&D on french fries alone.[2]

LARGE TOTAL ADDRESSABLE MARKET

While you may choose to target a specific niche segment to start with, it's important that the ultimate potential market be large. Obviously large means different things to different entrepreneurs, but you want to make sure that your market size matches your ambitions.

Tim Draper, legendary investor and early investor in Hotmail, was asked by Canada's *Globe and Mail* what his favorite metric is. He answered succinctly: "Market size. How big could the company become if it took the whole market?"[3]

One thing that is important to acknowledge is that sometimes the market will grow because your idea succeeded. Aaron Levine, a well-known entrepreneur who founded and is CEO of Box (a cloud-based enterprise storage provider), said recently on Twitter: "Sizing the market for a disruptor based on an incumbent's market is like sizing the car industry off how many horses there were in 1910."[4]

Sizing the opportunity is a real challenge in disruptive innovation. However, it doesn't make the exercise unnecessary. In the example above, with the benefit of hindsight, obviously looking at the percentage of all people over 16 would have been a much more significant input for sizing the automobile market.

A very famous example of the need to accurately size your market comes from a 1980 study that AT&T hired McKinsey & Company to conduct. AT&T's Bell Labs invented cellular technology, but was unsure how large the market for cell phones would be. McKinsey's study predicted 900,000 subscribers by 2000, so AT&T decided not to pursue cellular as a line of business.

McKinsey turned out (obviously) to be wrong. In fact, they were off by more than 100 times (the actual number of subscribers in 2000 was 109 million), and AT&T would later be forced to acquire McCaw Cellular for $12.6 billion to catch up in the cellular business.[5]

Bill Gurley referenced this case in a discussion on the size of Uber's total addressable market. A professor of finance at NYU's Stern School of Business, Aswath Damodaran, had estimated the size of the opportunity and ultimate likely valuation for Uber to be almost three times less than that predicted by early investor Gurley from Benchmark. Gurley noted several flaws in the professor's approach.

Specifically, Damodaran started his valuation estimation by looking at the existing taxi and car service market. Gurley on the other hand pointed out a half-dozen ways that Uber's experience and capabilities are far superior to the legacy taxi experience and therefore lead to a larger market than the existing one. Plus, he pointed out that some individuals are actually replacing car ownership—or at least replacing their extra vehicle—by using Uber. In his blog, "Above the Crowd," he explains: "Uber's potential market is far different from the previous for-hire market precisely because the numerous improvements over the traditional model lead to a greatly enhanced TAM [total available market]."[6] He also points to an interview he had with Uber's CEO in the *Wall Street Journal* in which he explained:

> When we got this company started (in 2009) we were pitching the seed round and we pulled a bunch of research from this report that showed that San Francisco total spend on taxi and limo was like 120 million bucks. But we're a very healthy multiple bigger than that right now, just Uber in SF. So it's not about the market that exists, it's about the market we're creating.[7]

TARGETING SPECIFIC CUSTOMER SEGMENTS TO START

While entrepreneurs may have a big vision, they will often choose to target specific customer segments to start with.

For example, when LinkedIn started out it focused on Silicon Valley technology leaders as its initial market. The founders began targeting their closest professional connections (roughly 350 people) to try the service, and then followed up with phone calls to those who didn't accept their invitation or take the next step of inviting their professional connections.[8]

Similarly, Tesla started with a narrow focus on its premium sports car, before expanding to other types of luxury vehicles with the Model S luxury sedan and most recently Model X SUV. You could imagine the company eventually continuing beyond premium vehicles toward a broad vision of serving everyone who drives a car.

As Martin Eberhard of Tesla explained to the *New York Times:* "Cell-phones, refrigerators, color TV's, they didn't start off by making a low-end product for masses . . . They were relatively expensive, for people who could afford it."

The companies that sold those products at first did so "not because they were stupid and they thought the real market was at the high end of the market," he said, but because that was how to get production started. He added that his company and others that have tried electric cars are too small to produce by the tens of thousands anyway.[9]

Tumblr took a similar approach. While the platform was open to any-one signing up, the company initially promoted it specifically as a place for artists to publish their work.[10] As the service grew, Tumblr was able to broaden that focus to include an expanded (although skewing younger) demographic by positioning everyone as a creative individual. Or as in-vestor Fred Wilson explained eloquently on his blog, "Tumblr is self ex-pression."[11] That was in November 2010 when, according to the digital analytics company comScore, page views had grown 1,540 percent over the previous year to 1.2 billion and unique US visitors had grown to six million per month (up 150 percent) with another eight million visitors from outside the US.[12]

Even with an ambitious vision, sometimes starting with a focus on the persona of the first customer can help greatly.

PUTTING THIS INTO ACTION

Question 1: How many people or companies could use the product or service being created?

It's tempting to answer "everyone" when asked this question. However, this is almost never the case. The ability to precisely and specifically define who your target customer is and then do research to understand how many of these individuals exist is critical to evaluating whether this business is ultimately worth the investment of your time and, potentially, your investor's money.

Generally, it's helpful to answer this question by coming up with three specific projections:

1. The *total addressable market* (or TAM), which is the universe of customers who could potentially use your service.
2. The *served available market* (or SAM), which is the universe of customers who you can reach with your current sales and marketing channels.
3. The *target market,* which is the number of your likely customers.

To illustrate it may be helpful to use as an example one of the companies we studied—Tesla. The TAM would be everyone who purchases a new car

Figure 3.1 Diagram of Market Types

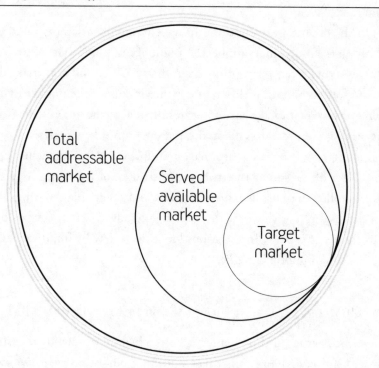

every year. Often, entrepreneurs break this number into two categories: (a) sales within the US and (b) sales to the rest of the world. The SAM might be limited initially to car sales in markets in which Tesla has a showroom and where customers are interested in electric vehicles. Finally, the target market would be restricted to include only those customers from the SAM who purchase high-end sports cars (at the time Tesla offered the Roadster) and later would be expanded to include buyers of luxury sedans (when Tesla released the Model S).

To come up with the numbers referred to in the list above you can use two techniques: top-down or bottom-up. It's often helpful to do both estimates and compare the results as a quick check to make sure your assumptions are reasonable.

To come up with a top-down number, you reference numbers found in third-party and analyst research. For example, a firm like Forrester Research or a sell-side analyst at an investment bank like Morgan Stanley may have issued a report that contains relevant market-sizing estimates. In the Tesla example, for instance, maybe they conducted research on the luxury sports car market.

On the other hand, a bottom-up review actually attempts to do direct analysis on the individual numbers. A point of caution is that research firms and analysts are often very optimistic in their analysis and may make different assumptions and draw different conclusions about the market than you would on your own. Make sure you carefully review the underlying assumptions driving their research if you depend on a top-down analysis.

Keep in mind some startups have multiple customer segments. For example, a lot of consumer Internet startups (like YouTube from our study) have the following customers: individuals and companies sharing videos, consumers watching these videos, and finally advertisers trying to deliver ads to those consumers. In situations like this, it may be important to estimate the size of multiple markets.

Question 2: Is there a niche I should focus on to start with?

As described earlier in this chapter, it's often helpful to start by focusing on a niche. Geoffrey Moore calls this a "bowling pin" strategy, in which you identify a niche customer segment from which you can later expand to include adjacent niches before ultimately dominating the entire market.

We referenced Tesla (high-end sports cars) and LinkedIn (Silicon Valley professionals) above when discussing this strategy, but no one may have applied this more brilliantly than Facebook—starting with a narrow focus on Harvard students and then strategically expanding to include more and more college students before finally opening the network up to everyone. The first bowling pin was Harvard, but as Facebook knocked that down it was able to easily use its density within that niche to find other, overlapping, niches.

Sometimes the niche is not a group of customers as much as it is part of the ultimate value being created. This is particularly common in network businesses, where the network isn't valuable until it has reached a critical density of customers. Tumblr is a good example of this in that many of its early customers used the service to easily post photos and other media quickly out to the Internet. However, Tumblr's long-term vision and, ultimately, a lot of the value individuals get from the service today, involve discovering interesting content on the platform from other authors.[13]

Question 3: Is there a good analogy you can use to frame the opportunity?

As in the case of Uber, there are situations in which a startup ends up creating a market. In these cases, it's often helpful to think through the disruption by analogy. While this isn't without risk, this technique is often used by startups in emerging markets who say, "I am the [insert successful startup] for [their target market]" when the successful startup effectively created a new market.

I have mixed feelings about this technique, as it's very often misused by entrepreneurs and VCs who are blindly following a trend.

For example, Airbnb's value proposition makes a ton of sense both to hosts and guests and has enabled the company to build a very successful business. Airbnb and Uber have popularized the concept of a "collaborative economy" in which individuals share their resources (homes or cars) and rent them, allowing their customers to forgo the often more costly services of a large company (hotel or car rental firms).

A lot of industries are being disrupted by this trend, and analysts like Jeremiah Owyang have done an excellent job covering it. However, a "collaborative economy" is not the right approach to solving every problem. Yet entrepreneurs are regularly pitching themselves as the Airbnb of [another industry]. While the idea of replicating Airbnb's success is exciting, the new companies rarely offer the same underlying value proposition. This leads to a false sense of security—hence the danger of this approach.

That said, if your target market has a lot of the same dynamics as the referenced successful startup had early in its development, it can be an effective technique to estimate a growing and hard-to-quantify market.

Question 4: How will I deliver my solution at scale? What efficiencies am I dependent on to achieve this?

It's important to understand how you are going to scale up your offering to delight customers. While some anticipated efficiences may be unproven, you should document these assumptions relative to the non-scalable techniques you may start with. I've found it's helpful to record them for two reasons: (a) it can clarify the goals for your team and (b) you may ultimately realize some of the hypotheses involve leaps of faith that you aren't comfortable making.

Thinking through these assumptions up front can decrease the chances your company ends up in a situation one growth equity investor likes to call "profitless prosperity." This is where your revenue continues to grow rapidly year over year, but the business never sees any of this growth lead to profits.

To avoid this, you want to pay particular attention to what are called your business's *unit economics*. These are the specific revenues and costs associated with your startup on a per unit (typically customer) basis. Per above, many of these per-customer costs will decrease as you scale the number of customers you are supporting, but you still should be able to account for these costs on a per-customer basis.

4

SOLVES A REAL PROBLEM

"The future is already here, it's just not very evenly distributed."

—William Gibson

IF YOU HAVE AN IDEA THAT YOU BELIEVE CAN SCALE, AND THE MARKET IS large enough to support your aspirations, the next step is to make sure that your product successfully solves a real problem for your target market.

This may feel like an obvious prerequisite, perhaps not even worthy of its own chapter. However, it actually turns out that a product's inability to meet the needs of its target market is a very common cause of startup failure. Perhaps no one has seen more early stage startups up close over the last ten years than Paul Graham, one of the co-founders of Y Combinator, which has funded over 800 startups, including, as mentioned in Chapter 1, Airbnb and Dropbox. In an essay he wrote on startup failure, he explains:

> In a sense there's just one mistake that kills startups: not making something users want. If you make something users want, you'll probably be fine, whatever else you do or don't do. And if you don't make something users want, then you're dead, whatever else you do or don't do.[1]

It's depressing that this is such a common failure point. It would be much better if most startups failed because they weren't successful in solving their technical challenges. That would make entrepreneurship and innovation a much more "fair" activity. The probability of success would be a simple function of the team's IQ and willingness to work long hours.

Over the last roughly half-dozen years, the lean startup movement has cataloged an entire set of techniques to help entrepreneurs learn from the market what it wants. As mentioned in the first chapter, if this concept is new to you I strongly encourage you to pick up Eric Reis's book *The Lean Startup* and Steve Blank's *Four Steps to the Epiphany.*

The element we want to focus on for this chapter is when you should focus on scaling and growth (the topic covered at length for the rest of this book). Again, this is the third of our four prerequisites: Before scaling, validate that your market cares deeply and will spend a meaningful amount of something valuable (often money, but sometimes attention) on the product you've built.

WHY DO ENTREPRENEURS OVERLOOK THE IMPORTANCE OF SOLVING A REAL PROBLEM?

Before we talk about when to move on to scale, we first need to discuss why this prerequisite is so often overlooked by entrepreneurs. As you start working on a problem, it's easy to rush quickly past the problem itself and shift your attention to the features of your product or service being developed.

A colleague at one of my first startups, Rob Vickery, liked to regularly remind me of the difference between a *feature* and *benefit* by explaining to me that every year, hundreds of thousands of homeowners go to the hardware store and buy drill bits. However, they aren't really purchasing just the drill bit. They are buying the future holes. In this example, the *feature* is a drill bit, and if you've ever walked into a Home Depot, you know there are plenty of different options for that feature. However, the *benefit* they are actually paying for is being able to drill the hole (or multiple holes) that result from this purchase.

In technology companies, failing to consider the benefit often means becoming very focused on the novel technology being developed to the detriment of its utility in the market. There is a famous VC cliché that "the best technology rarely wins." This is a cliché because so many dollars have been invested in startups with novel sets of technology features that ultimately fail to offer sufficient benefits to customers.

GOODNESS FACTOR

It's hard to get people to change their behavior. Don Jones, now deceased, a serial entrepreneur and venture investor in Pittsburgh, and the man for whom the Donald H. Jones Center for Entrepreneurship at Carnegie Mellon University is named, liked to challenge startups to concretely express the "goodness factor" of their idea. He defined this as a specific and quantified measurement of the improvement the startups' solution would deliver to a customer relative to the way the customers were currently solving the problem. Don determined that the new solution needed to be at least three times better than the current one to convert the user.

Being forced to think through and quantify the benefit is very important. People are ultimately lazier and more resistant to change than rational analysis would suggest. Therefore, solutions that are only slightly better than current practice will typically not prompt people to change.

A fascinating area of study at the moment is the field of behavioral economics, which explores why individuals make the choices they do, and why they make these choices even when they aren't, on paper, the most rational ones.

However, when launching a startup, we can't count on irrational actors. Fifteen years ago, when I was a young entrepreneur, Don Jones pushed me to quantify my goodness factor and make sure it was at least three times better.

Today, the bar has been raised as everyone is inundated with ever more marketing messages. Recently, Peter Thiel made a similar point about the need to have a quantified benefit relative to the competition but set the minimum benefit as being "at least ten times better than its closest substitute in some important dimension."[2]

He went on to explain how this applied to PayPal:

> PayPal, for instance, made buying and selling on eBay at least 10 times better. Instead of mailing a check that would take 7 to 10 days to arrive,

PayPal let buyers pay as soon as an auction ended. Sellers received their proceeds right away, and unlike with a check, they knew the funds were good.[3]

It's likely that the requirement for your "goodness factor" will rise even higher in the future.

HOW DO YOU VALIDATE THIS?

There is no substitute for customer feedback. However, you shouldn't wait to have an actual product to get feedback. You can start right now by talking to *prospective* customers.

Unfortunately, when you sit down and ask someone what they think about your idea, it's much harder than you might expect to get frank feedback. People are predisposed to tell you what they think you want to hear. It's how we're socialized.

No one wants to be the person to crush your dreams and reveal that your idea is a bad one. Paradoxically, the most valuable thing someone can do is provide frank feedback on your idea. Therefore, you have to make it easier for them to give you real, honest feedback—even if it's negative.

There are a number of techniques you can use to do this.

STORYBOARDS

While no one wants to crush your dream, people are comfortable collaborating on refining your preliminary ideas. The challenge is that you want them to give you thoughtful, constructive feedback, so you need to invest time in thinking through how your solution will work.

One technique that I've seen work really well is borrowed from Hollywood and other creative fields. They use a technique called a storyboard in which they use simplified graphics to illustrate what they are planning to create, be it a movie, play, or advertisement. A startup can use a similarly rendered storyboard to explain the problem faced by the customer, and then show how its proposed product or service will solve the problem and improve the customer's life afterward.

Use of a storyboard has worked for me in a number of situations to help solicit strong feedback from prospective customers because they feel much more comfortable being critical of something that is so clearly in an early stage of development.

Aaron Patzer, founder and CEO of Mint—one of the paired companies in our study—did a masterful job getting out and validating his problem before starting to develop the product. In a February 2011 lecture at Princeton University (from whose PhD program he had dropped out years earlier) he explained that he didn't write one line of code for the first three months of working on his idea, which was, originally, to create software that helped people set goals and then plan their lives based on the time and money required to accomplish those goals.

Aaron talked to everyone he could about the idea, and while the overall idea didn't resonate with people, the part about setting goals to manage their money did. Then as he dug in, he became convinced a large part of the problem with the tools currently available (at the time these would have been Intuit Quicken and Microsoft Money) was that they did not automatically categorize transactions. With his engineering background, he was able to experiment and quickly develop algorithms that categorized transactions reasonably well.

Aaron developed three alternative positioning statements and one-page descriptions of how the solution would work. He then took those statements and approached people waiting for CalTrain—the commuter train used by many Silicon Valley workers—to discuss his idea with them. As he pointed out in the Princeton lecture, this was a great way to avoid simply asking friends, and it allowed him to get responses from people who were more likely to be honest. He also was careful to avoid asking if they would use the program but instead judged the enthusiasm of their response to avoid the issues described above.

To this day, some of the positioning that is still key to Mint's success was discovered by using this approach. For example, the phrase "Bank Level Security," which was used during testing, turned out to be a key to getting people to trust a system like Mint with their finances. All of this testing was done before Mint had even created a website, yet it served to validate Aaron's idea.[4]

LAUNCH AS EARLY AS POSSIBLE

As noted above in the section discussing the goodness factor, there is, of course, a huge difference between what people imagine they'll do and what they actually do. Therefore, there is no substitute for watching customers interact with your product at some point.

In a keynote at the 2011 South by Southwest Interactive Festival, LinkedIn's Reid Hoffman explained ten rules for entrepreneurs. One of those rules, directly relevant to this prerequisite, is: "Launch early enough that you are embarrassed by your 1.0 product release."

He explained that he uses the term "embarrassed" intentionally, because all entrepreneurs want to unveil their product and have the market marvel at their brilliance. However, he added with a little humor, most of us are not Steve Jobs and are at least partially incorrect about the assumptions we have about what our customer really wants.

His speech continued with a great story from the early days of LinkedIn, when the company was launching the product. Reid had decided it was time to launch, but his co-founders pulled him into a room and explained they couldn't launch the service until they had built a key feature called "contact finder." After discussion, the team decided to launch the product without this feature, on the understanding and with the expectation that the feature would likely be the most requested thing from customers and the company would build it quickly. But the punch line was that at the time of Reid's lecture, eight years after launch, the team still wanted to build that feature but it had not yet become a high enough priority to actually do so.[5]

I think the fact the feature had not been built but still was on the road map really reinforces the point that no matter how smart a team is (and the LinkedIn founding team was as brilliant as any), the market is smarter. And, as Reid explained in his talk, it's also critical to get out of the building and on the street launching your product as soon as possible.

One comment about the terms used to describe these products: If you are familiar with the lean startup methodology, you'll know these early versions have been called an "MVP" or "minimally viable product."

I have no issue with the phrase MVP, as defined by Eric Reis, author of *Lean Startup:* "that version of a new product which allows a team to collect the maximum amount of validated learning about customers with the least effort."[6]

However, I think way too many entrepreneurs misinterpret "viable" as "sloppily put together." I believe the experience matters and frankly I've met with too many entrepreneurs over the years who mistakenly interpret a lack of demand for a product as a lack of interest in the concept itself when the lackluster demand was at least partially due to an ugly or unnecessarily complicated interface.

While an MVP should only contain the core features, allowing visionary customers to fill in the gaps, the product's essential benefits can't be realized if delivered through a horrible experience. We'll talk about this more in the next chapter, when we discuss the last prerequisite, creating a great user experience.

That's why I have given MVPs a new name and acronym, calling them Minimally Awesome Products (MAPs) instead of Minimally Viable Products. While some argue this is "just semantics," the vocabulary chosen matters when it impacts the expectations and goals toward which an entrepreneur aspires. You need the product to be awesome even with limited features if you really want to validate your assumptions about its ultimate success. The change in terminology also ends up providing a much better acronym, as these MAPs are really a way to *map* out the path toward your vision, although this is not why I started advocating the name change.

PUTTING AN EARLY LAUNCH INTO ACTION

Question 1: How many customers and potential customers have you talked to about your idea?

Steve Blank, serial entrepreneur turned educator and author, likes to tell entrepreneurs to "get out of the building." It's a very helpful reminder, as the lab or office is a comfortable place and it often feels easier to sit around a conference table and speculate about your customers' problems than to go out and talk to them.

However, no matter how smart you or your co-founders are, the market is much smarter. The key is to figure out who to talk to and how to shape that conversation.

If you're interested in getting quality feedback from customers you need to make sure the people you talk to are as unbiased as possible, and that they are part of your target market. For example, asking your friend what he or she thinks of your idea is unlikely to provide quality feedback. As mentioned earlier, friends won't want to crush your dreams.

Your friends can be helpful to you, but likely not via their feedback. Instead, get them to introduce you to friends of theirs who are target customers for your product or service.

Don't overlook the importance of having a clear target customer and how your solution will solve their problem. This should be clearly defined before you go have those conversations.

Then, when you sit down with potential customers, you can ask them quickly about themselves and discover up front if they have the problem your product solves. If you repeatedly find yourself talking to individuals who fit your profile but don't have the problem, you likely need to revise your idea or "pivot," as Eric Reis says. On the other hand, if the individuals don't fit your profile you don't need to be as concerned about their feedback. (Unless, of course, they are passionate about your solution, in which case you may want to discover whether they represent another good customer profile.)

Question 2: How satisfied are your current customers?

There are lots of different techniques you can use to understand your customers' satisfaction with a product once you have released a working version. A simple technique is to ask them how they feel about the value your solution delivers. Below, we'll review two specific survey techniques that can be applied to create a customer satisfaction score.

Net Promoter Score
Over the past few years the Net Promoter Score (or NPS®), a model for quantifying how customers feel about a product or business, has gained

significant attention. This model attempts to segment customers into three categories based on their answers to the following question on a zero-to-ten-point scale: *"How likely is it that you would recommend [your company] to a friend or colleague?"*

Those who answer with a rating of 9 or 10 are the "Promoters" and are key to the future of your growth because they will be loyal and refer other customers to your company or product. Those who answer below a rating of 6 are unhappy customers and will slow down your growth and tell others negative information. Those with ratings of 7 and 8 are in the middle and are unlikely to advocate for your solution but are currently satisfied and likely to stay with your company or product until a better solution comes along.

To calculate your score, take the percentage of customers who are Promoters (9 or 10) and subtract the percentage who are Detractors (below 6).[7]

Sean Ellis Model

Another technique comes from Sean Ellis, in collaboration with the startup website analytics company KISS Metrics. As mentioned in Chapter 1 of this book, Sean Ellis was one of the three individuals who coined the term "growth hacker" and has spent much of the last few years advancing the state of the art on how to think about marketing startups effectively to drive growth.

He created his own survey to analyze customer satisfaction. However, instead of asking about the likelihood that a customer would recommend the product or service, as the Net Promoter Score does, his survey asks customers how disappointed they'd be if the product was no longer available.

Specifically the question is: *"How would you feel if you could no longer use [product]?"*

1. Very disappointed
2. Somewhat disappointed
3. Not disappointed (it isn't really that useful)
4. N/A—I no longer use [product]

After analyzing hundreds of startups, he has determined that the benchmark to start focusing on scaling your offering is when at least 40 percent of your customers would be "very disappointed" if the product was no longer available.[8]

Question 3: What can you learn from analyzing customers you lost?

In addition to using the techniques described above to understand how satisfied your current customers are, you should also use another important technique and analyze the customers who have stopped using your product. This feedback is incredibly helpful in terms of showing both what originally caused a customer to sign up for your product or service and then later what led them to stop using it. In some cases, the explanation is as simple as they stopped needing whatever you are delivering. However, dig deeper to find the individuals who still have the problem you are solving but who have grown frustrated with your solution or found a better alternative.

In some situations—especially early in a company's development when you may not have that many customers who have discontinued the use of your product—it's also helpful to look at an analysis of lost sales. Instead of looking at people who signed up as customers and then stopped using your product or service, this approach involves looking at qualified leads, potential customers who start down a sales process with you and then stop before becoming customers. This method is also beneficial when customers sign long-term contracts up front, because in such cases you may not have a lot of customer turnover to analyze.

5

AN EXCELLENT FIRST
INTERACTION

"Art consists of limitation . . . The most beautiful part of every picture is the frame."

—G. K. Chesterton[1]

WILL ROGERS FAMOUSLY SAID, "YOU NEVER GET A SECOND CHANCE TO make a first impression." It turns out this is especially true for organizations focused on growth. The importance of a consumer's first interaction with a product is hard to overstate. Time is the most precious asset people have, and our attention spans are constantly shrinking, as more distractions compete for it. Therefore, a company needs to ensure the first drop of attention from a potential customer is rewarded with a great experience.

It's not news that people care about the first interaction with a product, but in our current media environment it has become more obvious *how much* people care about it. One of the most popular types of videos on YouTube are called "unboxing" videos, which, in essence, show someone taking a product out of its box and describing it to the YouTube audience. In 2013, according to CNN, "2,370 days, or 6.5 years, worth of unboxing footage was uploaded to the site."[2] These videos aren't just being uploaded en masse, they are being watched—a lot! One of the most popular channels for unboxing videos is DisneyCollector, a YouTube channel focused on kids toys.

In an article about a 21-year-old creator of unboxing videos, the *New York Times* explained:

> Her most popular clip to date has the abstruse but keyword-dense title "Angry Birds Toy Surprise Jake and the Never Land Pirates Disney Pixar Cars 2 Easter Egg SpongeBob." At last check, it had garnered more than 90 million hits. To put that into perspective: It's as if every child under age 5 in the United States has seen it. Four times. This past July, Disney-Collector's YouTube channel became the most-watched one in the United States.[3]

Before we write this off as a children's phenomenon, high-end electronics and handbags are also extremely popular categories for unboxing videos. And don't forget about the almost billion-dollar cable television channel HGTV. The network has delivered consistent and growing ratings over almost 20 years by producing many variations on the basic concept first introduced with their anchor program—*House Hunters*. The basic concept is to give viewers a peek inside another family's real-estate transaction and then, in many cases, allow viewers to watch as the property goes through the process of renovation that concludes as new homeowners walk through the house for the first time.

A 2014 article in the *Los Angeles Times* profiling HGTV's success concluded:

> HGTV also continues to find still more ways to recycle the inexpensive "House Hunters" formula with shows such as "Living Alaska," "Beachfront Bargain Hunt" and "Island Hunters" featuring property quests in exotic locales.
>   "We call it 'property porn,'" said Drew Scott of "Property Brothers." "That's what people want to see. They'll never get sick of it."[4]

Yes, the modern media landscape certainly provides a lens into the importance we place on the first interaction with a product. In this context, we'll focus the rest of this chapter on two best practices for thinking through a first interaction.

CREATING CONSTRAINTS

Often, by adding constraints to a product, you can ensure that the essence of the product experience is a positive one. Anyone who has played a multiple-level video game has experienced this on an individual basis. In a well-designed game, users progress through levels, adding complexity and difficulty throughout. This ensures the initial interaction is positive, and also one with which players will not quickly grow bored.

In many of the companies studied, executives constrained the product or market in the early days of its development to ensure a similarly positive first experience. Facebook may be the most obvious example of this. As most people know, Facebook initially restricted access to its network to students at Harvard, before expanding to include students at other specific colleges and universities and then to all college students (and finally, to everyone).

This seems to run counter to broadly accepted principles of creating any new communication network. Whether we are talking about a phone, fax machine, or, in this case, a social network, the network is obviously unusable until more than one person starts using it. On the other hand, as individuals join the network, it becomes more valuable with each additional node on the network. This is often modeled mathematically as the perceived value of the network being the number of connected individuals or devices on that network squared. Bob Metcalfe, the inventor of Ethernet and founder of 3Com, famously first presented this framework, so it is referred to as Metcalfe's Law. We'll come back to network theory again in Chapter 14.

For the purpose of this discussion, it's worth just pointing out that given this calculation of value, it would have seemed to be important to add as many users as possible to the Facebook network as quickly as possible. However, it turns out that a more accurate way to frame the principle is that connections are only valuable to potential customers if they find the other people who have joined interesting to connect with.

Speaking at a conference in 2003, just months before Facebook was founded, Internet expert Clay Shirky commented about social software:

> Scale alone kills conversations, because conversations require dense two-way conversations. In conversational contexts, Metcalfe's Law is a drag.

The fact that the amount of two-way connections you have to support goes up with the square of the users means that the density of conversation falls off very fast as the system scales even a little bit. You have to have some way to let users hang onto the less is more pattern, in order to keep associated with one another.

This is an inverse value to scale question. Think about your Rolodex. A thousand contacts, maybe 150 people you can call friends, 30 people you can call close friends, two or three people you'd donate a kidney to. The value is inverse to the size of the group. And you have to find some way to protect the group within the context of those effects.[5]

Shirky goes on to talk about solutions developed at the time by other social software companies, but in my opinion, Facebook's solution just months later was much more elegant. By limiting the community first to students at specific schools and then to college students at large, Mark Zuckerberg found a way to ensure that his community had a high density of conversations as the Facebook network scaled.

It actually took Facebook three times longer to get to one million users than Friendster (ten months vs three months), even though Facebook was launched a few years later and theoretically there was more infrastructure (penetration of desktop computers with Internet access) available. However, Facebook's early constraint ensured a powerful experience which laid the foundation for significant later growth.[6]

Dan Olsen, the former senior director of product at Friendster, commented to CNET that, from his point of view, this deliberate rolling out of who could sign up was the most important part of Facebook's strategy: "I don't know if they did it deliberately, but they started at one US college campus, then another, then another . . . When you control your roll out like that, you can control scale."[7]

Facebook's focus on creating great experiences for its customers went so far as to impact the semantics Facebook used to describe visitors to the site. In his book on his time at Facebook, early employee (number 30) Noah Kagan explained that Facebook founder Mark Zuckerberg had six "laws." The first of these was:

Never say the word "user." Ever. Mark would literally yell at you for using this word. It mattered to him and still sticks with me to this day.
He wanted us to recognize the users as people, not just a user, which he
thought was belittling.[8]

Another good example comes from Twitter. The company was often mis-
understood, and its platform was even ridiculed in the early days, as Twitter
had decided to artificially restrict the platform, not by limiting who could
sign up but instead by limiting the length of the messages and by not adding
a number of what seemed like obvious features, such as the ability to add for-
matting to updates. This restriction ended up encouraging individuals to publish thoughts much more quickly, resulting in real-time value for the network.

In 2007, one of the Twitter founders, Evan Williams, gave a presentation at the Web 2.0 Summit, in which he encouraged developers to add
constraints to their products and reduce the "cognitive load." He contrasted
the simplicity of Twitter with an early publishing platform he helped create,
Blogger (ultimately acquired by Google), noting that when he introduced
features like subject lines, it encouraged users to hesitate before publishing.[9]

Another company that skillfully reduced the "cognitive load" of its product is Google. When contrasted with other search engines at the time it was
starting, the Google interface was shockingly simple. The screenshots below
contrast the home pages of Yahoo![10] and Google[11] three months after Google
launched.

One final entrepreneur from our study who was passionate about using
constraints to create a great first-user experience was Ray Kroc. In his autobiography, he describes the first time he saw the first McDonald's (started
by the two brothers with whom he would later partner and then ultimately
buy the business from):

I was fascinated by the effectiveness of the system they [the McDonald
brothers] described that night. Each step in producing the limited menu
was stripped down to its essence and accomplished with minimal effort.[12]

Kroc was so committed to simplicity and the experience of great food
that he made a very controversial decision at the time: to prohibit franchise

Figure 5.1 Yahoo vs. Google

operators from placing pay phones, jukeboxes, and vending machines in the restaurants. In his autobiography he explains the rationale:

> Many times operators have been tempted by the side income some of these machines offer, and they have questioned my decision. But I've stood firm. All of those things create unproductive traffic in a store and encourage loitering that can disrupt your customers.[13]

Even today, in a discussion of the company's history on the McDonald's corporate website, Kroc's philosophy, his ultimate goal, is described as follows:

Ray Kroc wanted to build a restaurant system that would be famous for food of consistently high quality and uniform methods of preparation. He wanted to serve burgers, buns, fries and beverages that tasted just the same in Alaska as they did in Alabama.[14]

The constraints of limited and consistent menus ensured that each of the franchises would deliver a delightful experience for customers from the first time they walked through the Golden Arches.

PRODUCT ARCHITECTURE CHOICES

It's easy to assume these product choices are limited to the surface-level aspects of how a product looks and feels. However, in the examples we studied, we came to appreciate that this was far from the case. We realized that in addition to a simple product design, the companies that achieved scale often had architectural advantages as well.

For example, in the case of WordPress, the decision to use the programming language PHP instead of Perl allowed a much simpler installation process. In a reflective blog post analyzing "How did WordPress win?" Byrne Reese, the former product manager for Movable Type, comments,

> The fact that WordPress has always been easy to install, especially when compared to Movable Type, has always played a significant role in its growth and adoption rate. Technically, the reasons behind WordPress' famed 5-minute install can be attributed largely to PHP's deployment model, which was architected specifically to address the challenges associated with running and hosting web applications based on CGI, or in effect Perl—the Internet's first practical web programming language.
>
> Furthermore, every web host likes to configure CGI differently on their web server, which led to a lot of confusion and frustration for a lot of users, and prevented anyone from authoring a simple and canonical installation guide for all Movable Type users across all web hosts.
>
> One cannot underestimate how important ones installation experience with a piece of software is, because it frames every subsequent experience and impression they have of the product. So while blogging was

exploding and people were weighing their options between Movable Type and WordPress, it's no wonder why increasingly more and more people chose WordPress, even though it had fewer features, and an inferior design. Fewer people gave up trying to install it.[15]

In the case of Mint versus Wesabe, one of the biggest reasons for Wesabe's failure was its decision not to use a third-party service called Yodlee, a company that provides automatic financial data aggregation as a Web service. Mint chose to use Yodlee, allowing its users to have a simpler experience because Yodlee would quickly collect the user's bank data. As in the case of WordPress's easy installation, the importance of the ease and positivity of a user's first experience with Mint cannot be underestimated.

At the time, Wesabe felt that it was not a good idea to use Yodlee, and instead sought to create its own data-harvesting program to ensure more accurate data. Despite the potentially more accurate results, Wesabe's program created more initial work for the user. Mint's relationship with Yodlee allowed its users to simply connect to their bank accounts and start to experience beautiful graphs about their finances. Wesabe, in the words of one of the founders, "sucked at that" (a statement made in a postmortem blog post after shutting down the service).[16]

FRIENDSTER

The team at Friendster started out well; it quickly raised capital and had many top-tier venture investors join its board. Unfortunately, in hindsight, that group of investors became focused on things beyond creating a great experience. Russel Siegelman, a partner at one of these investment funds, the legendary Kleiner Perkins Caufield & Byers, admitted to the *New York Times:*

> All of a sudden Jonathan [founder of Friendster] had all these high-powered investors to please . . . He had all this money in the bank, so there was all this pressure to hire people and get things done. Open up new territories: China, Japan, Germany. Add all these new features. Meantime, he took his eye off the ball.[17]

In the same article, Kent Lindstrom, then Friendster's president, elaborated:

> They were talking about the next thing. Voice over Internet. Making
> Friendster work in different languages. Potential big advertising deals. Yet
> we didn't solve the first basic problem: our site didn't work.[18]

While he declined to talk to the *New York Times,* Jonathan Abrams later
gave an interview to the online news site *Mashable* in which he acknowledged the company had plans to build a college-focused network within
Friendster and also add a lot of the features that later drove great engagement on the Facebook platform. He explained, "The fact that we didn't
launch those products was a problem, but even more fundamentally, people
could barely log into the website for two years."[19]

Melissa Gilbert, the company's first investor, explained in the *New York
Times* article:

> Friendster ended up with three levels of VP's, CEO's and board members
> who, although they had great résumés, they were not connected to the
> social networking concept and didn't really use Friendster.[20]

From engineering architects at Wesabe and Six Apart/Movable Type
to the board at Friendster, these first illustrations reveal a theme that will
recur throughout this entire book: Everyone in the organization needs to be
focused on making decisions that support the company's growth.

PUTTING THIS INTO ACTION

Question 1: How many customers have you watched interact with your product?

Watching users interact with your product is a surprisingly powerful process. At all stages of a product's development, the insights derived from this
simple test often surprise entrepreneurs who don't have experience with the
technique. There are a number of approaches that can be taken, but rather

than walk users through the system, telling them how to accomplish the goal, the key is that you sit back and watch as they try to accomplish specific goals on the system.

This process often leads to the realization that layouts and interaction patterns, which felt obvious to the inventors of the system, are viewed as hidden or counterintuitive to the user. Similarly, instructions that inventors felt were crystal clear end up being quite ambiguous to potential customers.

When you reach the point at which your focus shifts to growth, it becomes especially important to focus on user studies around the first interaction. A few specific experiments that I've found to be particularly powerful in this area are the 15- or 30-second test and the setup test.

In the 15- or 30-second test, you simply show users the product in its full packaging, if it's a physical product, or start users on the home page or app store download page of a digital product for only (not surprisingly) 15 or 30 seconds and then take the product away. Ask the users simple questions like the following:

- What does the product do?
- How could you imagine using it?
- What would you do first?

What often emerges from this test is that the benefits are not clear to the user, and neither are they clear on how to start using it. Also, as discussed above, it may become obvious that there are too many options being presented.

After that, give the product back to the users and ask them to use it to accomplish whatever goal would be typical in a first-use case (e.g., set up an account and post your first message). It can be painful to watch them struggle as they attempt to do this. However, don't jump in and help them. Unless you plan to be personally on board for all of your customers forever, which will certainly limit your growth rate, keep in mind that many of your other potential customers may be experiencing similar confusion.

One question that often comes up is how many usability tests should be run. The answer is surprising. The best practice is to run no more than five at any single point, but as you change things, you should quickly run through new iterations of the five tests. Jakob Nielsen, one of the experts in the field, published research in 2000 that concludes, "Elaborate usability tests are a waste of resources. The best results come from testing no more than five users and running as many small tests as you can afford." He explains later in the same essay, "After the fifth user, you are wasting your time by observing the same findings repeatedly but not learning much new."[21]

Question 2: Where does your customer encounter friction?

As you start summarizing the results of these first interaction tests, the need for some changes will be obvious and many of these changes can be made quickly. Others will require more effort and analysis in order to make the necessary iterations to improve the initial interaction.

It's often helpful to map out the processes that you observe and highlight specific areas of friction that emerge. For example, in the cases referenced above, Byrne Reese talked about how Movable Type had different installation patterns depending on which web host the bloggers chose to use for their site. Depending on the host, a blogger's CGI (Common Gateway Interface) would be configured differently, and therefore, the setup steps necessary would also be unique. When you encounter an area of friction, brainstorm ways to remove it by adding constraints or, when necessary, changing the architecture.

Question 3: What experiments can you run to test improvements?

As you make larger changes to your users' first interactions with the product it's helpful, whenever possible, to test the impact by breaking your users into separate cohorts and studying how the changes impact the long term. Sometimes, for a variety of reasons, this isn't possible, but at a minimum, you should use rolling cohorts on a monthly basis to track how engagement with your product changes.

An interesting public example of this was done by Robert Moore on Twitter's users on *TechCrunch* right after Twitter raised $100 million. Moore explained the results.

Each line in the chart below represents a different "cohort" of Twitter users based on the month they joined (we chose seven cohorts from different time periods to avoid clutter). In the chart below, we monitor what percent of the users in each cohort come back to tweet again in each month after having tweeted in the first month. Obviously, month 1 is 100 percent by definition.

One of his conclusions from this analysis is as follows:

The newer cohorts, despite being significantly larger in size, actually consist of more loyal users. The two highest lines are also the two most recent, meaning that *users who joined in 2009 are actually more likely to keep tweeting after their first month than those who joined in the same month in 2008.*[22]

Figure 5.2 Cohort Analysis of Twitter Users

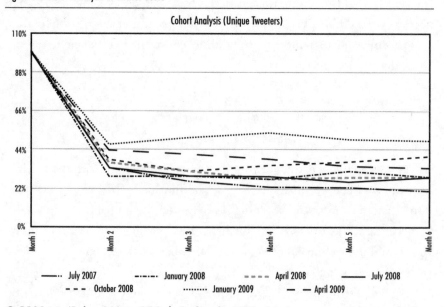

© *RJ Metrics/Robert Moore, CEO & Co-founder RJMetrics*

Your goal should be similar, to improve user experience and loyalty with each iteration, and doing a cohort analysis is a very effective way to ensure your changes are working.

Finally, as you step back and start the process of analyzing your customer's first interactions with your product, it can seem like there is nothing significant enough to hold back your growth. Don't fall into this trap. It's often a series of small changes, compounded, that are needed to create the growth curve you desire.

Question 4: Does it make sense to create a guided tour of your solution?

In situations where a salesperson or customer service person can't walk customers through their first interaction, it's often helpful to think about how prompts might be used to guide them through the first experience with a product.

The use of guides built into the product has become increasingly popular with software applications and websites in recent years. Product designer Andrew Coyle explains:

> Incorporating a guided tour helps a user understand an app's features and functions. A guided tour is usually presented during first time use, and can also be in context of screens discovered in later use. The tour helps the user learn how to use the app by providing an overview of important functions. The overview is usually presented in the form of an overlay or through coach marks. An overlay is a veil casted over an application with a dialog box containing product information. Coach marks are markers that are temporarily placed next to features that show a message when clicked or tapped.[23]

While it's easiest to think about these guided tours in the context of digital products, they can also be applied to physical products, by thinking through the process customers go through when they take a product out of the box.

Congratulations! Now that you've successfully optimized your user's first interaction, you've completed the necessary four prerequisites— the founder's core vision, scalable ideas, solves a real problem, excellent first interaction— and can start focusing on scaling up your innovation!

SECTION II

CATALYSTS FOR ACCELERATING GROWTH

ONCE YOU HAVE SATISFIED THE FOUR PREREQUISITES DESCRIBED IN THE preceding chapters, your attention should shift to growing as quickly as the business will allow. Of course, there will still be constraints on that growth. For example, how much cash you are able to invest or simply how many customers you are able to support and still provide an excellent experience.

However, you need to start searching for catalysts to accelerate growth. On its website, the American Chemical Society explains the term *catalyst* as follows:

> A catalyst makes a reaction happen. In a process known as catalysis, a relatively small amount of foreign material, called a catalyst, augments the rate of a chemical reaction without being consumed in the reaction. A catalyst can make a reaction go faster and in a more selective manner. Because of its ability to speed up some reactions and not others, a catalyst enables a chemical process to work more efficiently and often with less waste.[1]

For entrepreneurs or even large companies looking to commercialize a new product, using some of the techniques in this section can help their innovations reach critical mass "faster and in a more selective manner."

The next four chapters provide four best practices to think about as you try to catalyze this growth. To be clear, unlike the four prerequisites in the preceding section, all of which had to be checked off before proceeding, not every startup will need to take advantage of all the best practices. However, these techniques should be in every entrepreneur's tool kit for consideration.

6

DOUBLE TRIGGER EVENTS

"People do not buy goods and services. They buy relations, stories and magic."

—Seth Godin[1]

CLARIFYING MISCONCEPTIONS OF THE BIG LAUNCH

As we discussed in Chapter 2, a founder's core vision, in hindsight, will typically look obvious. However, at the time the founders embark on their journey their vision is often a truth that many others don't yet realize. It's therefore tempting to think that the key to success is to find a big enough stage or platform on which to unveil your solution. However, as students of the lean entrepreneurship movement hear repeatedly, it's usually not a good idea to launch your product with a "big bang."[2] This is solid counsel from my experience.

Although this is solid counsel on day one of a startup, it may not be such sage advice later on. One thing we repeatedly noticed in our study, across many of our chosen companies, was that some successful startups built awareness by drafting off larger events to catalyze growth once they had completed the four prerequisites described in section one.

Later, many of these events seem to be considered the startup's "launch," advancing the misconception that a big bang launch is a prerequisite for success. In none of the companies we analyzed is this more apparent than Twitter.

I've been attending the South by Southwest (SxSW) conferences since before Twitter's breakout year in 2007. And every year since 2007, journalists rush home to talk about the next thing to launch at SxSW, and ask whether [insert startup name here] is the next Twitter. It's a great narrative for these journalists, especially when you consider Twitter is today worth over $21 billion. This story of SxSW launching Twitter has dramatically increased the popularity of the SxSW Interactive Festival and become startup folklore. Unfortunately, it's not actually true that Twitter was launched at SxSW. As described by Evan Williams on Quora, here is what actually happened (emphasis mine):

> . . . contrary to common belief, **we didn't actually launch Twitter at SXSW**—SXSW just chose to blow it up. We launched it nine months before—to a whimper. By the time SXSW 2007 rolled around, we were starting to grow finally and it seemed like all of our users (which were probably in the thousands) were going to Austin that year. So, we did two things to take advantage of the emerging critical mass:
>
> 1. We created a Twitter visualizer and negotiated with the festival to put flat panel screens in the hallways. This is something they'd never done before, but we didn't want a booth on the trade show floor, because we knew hallways is where the action was. We paid $11K for this and set up the TVs ourselves. (This was about the only money Twitter's *ever* spent on marketing.)
> 2. We created an event-specific feature, where, you could text "join sxsw" to 40404. Then you would show up on the screens. And, if you weren't already a Twitter user, you'd automatically be following a half-dozen or so "ambassadors," who were Twitter users also at SXSW. We advertised this on the screens in the hallways. (I don't know how many people signed up this way—my recollection is not a lot.)
>
> I don't know what was the most important factor, but networks are all about critical mass, so doubling down on the momentum seemed like a good idea. And something clicked.[3]

When we look through the cases we've analyzed, this pattern of a product or service launching and then later having a big event "to blow it up" appears to be common. As we started looking at these later events, we started calling them a "double trigger"—the first trigger was getting the product in the market and getting feedback, but this second event was the double trigger that ultimately catalyzed growth. I'd like to highlight three types of events that can have this catalyzing impact.

DOUBLE TRIGGER TYPE 1:
SOMETHING HAPPENS TO YOUR PRODUCT

In December 2005, *Saturday Night Live* aired a digital short called "Lazy Sunday" starring Andy Samberg and Chris Parnell. The video was a hit on *SNL* and was uploaded to YouTube shortly after it aired. While eventually the video was pulled at NBC Universal's request (for copyright reasons), this didn't happen until February, after over seven million views of the video on YouTube's service. When website analytic vendors like HitWise plot the growth of YouTube's traffic, you can easily see the day in December 2005 when "Lazy Sunday" started accelerating growth dramatically. That increase in growth wasn't short lived, but in fact continued from that point forward.[4]

Based on that impact, Rick Cotton, chief counsel of NBC Universal, argued at an industry event that NBC ultimately made YouTube worth $1.5 billion. While that seems a bit extreme, the popularity of "Lazy Sunday" certainly catalyzed YouTube's growth. As a reminder, at the point Rick Cotton made the claim, Google had recently acquired YouTube for $1.5 billion.

DOUBLE TRIGGER TYPE 2:
A BIG EVENT NEEDS YOUR PRODUCT

In 2008, the Democratic Party made the decision to move Obama's speech at their convention in Denver from the Pepsi Center (capacity 18,007) to the larger outdoor venue of Invesco Field (capacity 76,125). The decision immediately created logistical challenges, as there simply were not enough hotels in Denver to handle the expected additional visitors, but it created a catalyst for Airbnb.

Later *CNN Money* reported on that accommodation crisis moment:

> For Airbnb co-founder Brian Chesky, that was a Eureka moment.
>
> "We were thinking to ourselves . . . light bulb's going off," he said. "That's where they're going [to] stay: They're going [to] stay at Airbnb homes."
>
> In a matter of weeks, hundreds of people started listing their Denver apartments on Airbnb for visitors to rent. Airbnb allows users to rent out everything from an extra room to a separate home.
>
> "Had it not been for the DNC, it's hard to know what Airbnb would be today," Chesky told CNNMoney. "These things, it's hard to get them going and you need a big kind of pop."[5]

While LinkedIn held off on all PR until it had 40,000 members and had already raised its first round of institutional financing from Sequoia Capital, once the company started its PR, it used a similar strategy to Airbnb. Instead of focusing on the overall service and how it worked, LinkedIn would pitch reporters on stories about members who found a job through LinkedIn. The company also rolled out the PR primarily through local media channels and focused on successful job searches in the home city of the reporter to whom the company was making a pitch This allowed LinkedIn to present the value of its platform and the LinkedIn experience to the press as something much more concrete.[6]

DOUBLE TRIGGER TYPE 3:
A COMPETITOR MAKES A MISTAKE

Sometimes the event that acts as a catalyst is actually a misstep by a competitor. To me, the case of Movable Type vs WordPress is actually one of the most interesting examples of an event catalyzing growth. Specifically, Movable Type's May 2004 decision to change the terms of its license.

In a *Forbes* magazine story eight years later, reviewing WordPress's early history, author J. J. Colao explained:

In a field dominated by Movable Type, their service [WordPress] attracted thousands of users through word of mouth. After Movable Type's owners decided to charge users in 2004, WordPress attracted a deluge of incensed refugees fleeing the company. By that August WordPress boasted 15,000 users and a pack of loyal developers refining code for free around the world.[7]

As Movable Type Product Manager Byrne Reese explained in his blog postmortem later:

> . . . what users feared most of all, is a repeat of exactly what happened the day Movable Type announced its licensing change: one day waking up to the realization that you owe some company hundreds, if not thousands of dollars and not being able to afford or justify the cost monetarily or on principle.[8]

It's clear that Byrne is absolutely right. When you go back now and look at the early reaction, that fear is clear, and WordPress definitely used it to their advantage. For example, Ari Paparo, now a startup CEO and at the time an Internet marketing consultant, wrote a post titled "Time to Update the PowerPoint" in which he said:

> As part of my consulting work I've implemented several corporate blogs, both as intranet and external solutions. In every case, I pitched some of the big advantages to MT:
>
> - Low cost license
> - Flexible, no restrictions
> - Easy to create multiple blogs
> - Easy to add new users
>
> Well, that's all shot to hell.[9]

It would be easy to misinterpret the recommendations of this chapter as: Just work hard and hope you get lucky with a large event. Instead, I think you need to take the steps described to look for opportunities to exploit.

The section below will review ways you can systematically explore these opportunities.

PUTTING THIS INTO ACTION

Question 1: Are there any places, times of year, or events where your customers are much more likely than usual to have the problem your product solves?

Once you identify the times of year or events when your customers can most use your product, figure out how you can tell a story—or recruit media to help you tell a story—to make those customers aware of your solution during this peak pain point.

A business that was one of my earliest venture investments is particularly good at this. The company is called NoWait, and has developed an iPad application that allows casual dining restaurants (those that still offer table service but not reservations, like Chili's and Buffalo Wild Wings) to manage crowds of waiting diners without using those awful legacy buzzer systems. It also allows consumers who dine at those restaurants to see the wait time and get in line remotely, using the service via a separate iPhone or Android application. As an investor, I'm biased, but it's a magical experience to get in line from home on a busy Friday night and simply walk in the door just as my table is ready. At the moment, over 230 million guests have experienced this at thousands of different restaurants who use our service. And the company is growing rapidly, so by the time this book is printed it will definitely be much larger.

However, the company hasn't always had such a dominant position. After satisfying each of the prerequisites with an early set of a few hundred customers the business was looking for ways to amplify awareness and catalyze growth.

As part of the 2013 Masters Golf Tournament the company partnered with the Mayor of Augusta, Deke Copenhaver, to get local restaurants to use its solution during the tournament. To help accelerate commitments, for every Augusta restaurant that agreed to use the service, NoWait would make a donation to the Wounded Warrior Foundation of Augusta.

More importantly, as Mayor Copenhaver explained: "Every April, Augusta overflows with hungry golf fans. It's an exciting time and one where we believe technology like NoWait's can reduce the normal stress and frustration of waiting in line for a table."[10] You see, it turns out that for most of the year Augusta is a normal Georgia town with most of the Augusta National Golf Club members who come in for a visit simply dining at the club. However, once a year during the Masters the local restaurants end up filling up with guests who come to town to watch the professionals play. These are casual dining restaurants and they are packed full, with long waits to get in. For example, the Hooters in Augusta actually flies in additional waitresses and pitches tents in the parking lot to handle all of the guests.

Well, fifty restaurants later that year at the Masters, NoWait was the talk of the tournament. The company was able to attract national media attention and catch the eye of key restaurant chain executives who had come to town to visit their busy locations and possibly check in on the golf as well.

Question 2: What can you do to develop communication competencies internally to be ready to respond when opportunities present themselves?

Looking back on the WordPress/Movable Type licensing fiasco, it was clear that WordPress (Automattic) had developed the competencies to be able to clearly and quickly respond when an opportunity presented itself.

Both companies maintained a blogging platform and had leadership teams that maintained public blogs, so it was second nature for them to engage this way. In fact, it was a blog post by Mena Trott, the co-founder of Movable Type/Six Apart, that was "ground zero" for an explosive online discussion that opened:

COMMITMENT TO A FREE VERSION,
WHILE GETTING OUR PRICING RIGHT
As I hope you already know, today we launched the Movable Type 3.0 Developer Edition, what you may not know is that with this release we are also making major improvements in our licensing and support policies.[11]

That post had a feature common to many blogging platforms (including Movable Type) called a "trackback" which allowed bloggers writing in reaction to a post to automatically enable a link to their article and relevant excerpt at the bottom of the original post. The trackbacks on this post show how negatively and quickly the community responded.

Mena published the post at 2:31 a.m. on May 13. The first of the blog posts in response, titled "Looks Like I'll Be Dumping MovableType Soon," was written less than three hours later, at 5:03 a.m. Over the next 24 hours, the post received 325 incoming links from other blogs, almost all of which were complaining about the changes, including several emotional posts like "I Feel Like I've Been Stabbed in the Back" and a number that used creative wordplay like "Mutinous Type," "Movable Type Commits 'Typicide,'" and "SixaPAY."[12]

One of the posts that first day was from Automattic founder Matt Mullenweg, a simple paragraph in which he explained:

> Our friends at Six Apart have announced their new pricing scheme. Best of luck to them moving forward and growing as a business. I have been receiving emails all morning asking if I have any plans to charge for WordPress in the future. The answer is no, but my answer doesn't matter. The license WordPress is distributed under—the GNU Public License— ensures that the full source is available free of charge, legally.[13]

Figure 6.1 Movable Type Fiasco Timeline

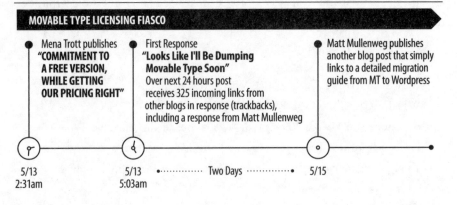

On May 15, Matt followed up with another short post, this time linked to a very detailed blog post by a frustrated Movable Type customer with detailed instructions on how to migrate to WordPress.[14] The linked post starts: "Mena says it's about time, and I can't agree more. It's about time Movable Type users moved to WordPress."[15]

As the timeline in Figure 6.1 illustrates, this moved quickly.

Obviously, years later we have the benefit of 20/20 hindsight. However, it's clear that Matt struck the appropriate tone in these responses and getting the right tone was driven by his communication competencies.

DRAFTING OFF PLATFORMS

"Coming together is a beginning; keeping together is progress; working together is success."

—Henry Ford

WHEN AND HOW TO THINK ABOUT BUSINESS DEVELOPMENT

In the last chapter, I tried to clarify some misconceptions around big launch events. I think many entrepreneurs are similarly confused about where and how to think about partnerships when scaling up their startup. In 140 characters, they get sage advice like: "For startups the default answer to biz dev deals should be no. They almost never turn out to be worth the distraction" (Paul Graham, founder of Y Combinator, on Twitter).[1]

When thinking about business development in the "classic" sense (sitting in windowless conference rooms across the country, delivering Power-Point presentations) it's hard to argue with Paul's advice above.

However, a great question for entrepreneurs to ask themselves, once they have satisfied the prerequisites described in the first section of this book, is: *Where are large groups of engaged potential customers, who are frustrated because they aren't aware of my solution, spending time today?* If you can tap into one of these communities of frustration, you can catalyze rapid growth.

PayPal Drafting off eBay

In his Stanford course CS 183 and again in his book *Zero to One,* Peter
Thiel explained how one company can draft off another in his description
of PayPal's growth:

> The first high-growth segment was power buyers and power sellers on
> eBay. These people bought and sold a ton of stuff. The high velocity of
> money going through the system was linked to the virality of customer
> growth. By the time people understood how and why PayPal took off on
> eBay, it was too late for them to catch up. The eBay segment was locked
> in. And the virality in every other market segment—e.g., sending money
> to family overseas—was much lower. Money simply didn't move as fast in
> those segments. Capturing segment one and making your would-be com-
> petitors scramble to think about second- and third-best segments is key.[2]

While the impact of aligning itself with eBay was certainly impressive,
it's interesting to back up and hear the PayPal founders talk about the "pivots" the company had to go through to get to that point. Reid Hoffman,
later the founder of LinkedIn but earlier in his career an executive VP at
PayPal, did an interview with *Fast Company* in which he explained the five
"pivots" (a term from the lean startup movement that refers to iterations
in the vision of your product or service) the company went through before
starting to focus on email payments and then discovering the growth engine
that eBay buyers and sellers ultimately provided.

Specifically, PayPal started out around novel encryption technology
geared toward mobile phones. As the company started investigating how to
commercialize that technology, it focused on payments from mobile phones
and then moved from phones to the PalmPilot platform. As PayPal became
suspicious of the PalmPilot use case the company decided to expand by offering to do payments via email and put both the PalmPilot platform and
the email platform in the market to see which use case resonated more with
its customers.[3] In January 2000, both products had about 12,000 customers. Yet by September of 2000, the email offering had roughly four million
customers and the Palm product still had about 12,000, making it obvious

which product to focus on.[4] This quick growth was driven primarily by
the rapid adoption of the payment method on the eBay platform. However, what's interesting is that the PayPal team's initial reaction, according
to Reid, was "What is this eBay thing?" But they quickly realized, "Oh my
gosh, these are our customers" and set out to optimize that use case.[5]

YouTube Drafting off MySpace
Authors Putting Videos on Page

The founders of YouTube (who earlier in their career were at PayPal) obviously took this lesson of drafting off of existing platforms to heart.

A lot of YouTube's growth came from MySpace users embedding You-
Tube videos on their MySpace pages. In fact, the month before YouTube
was acquired by Google for $1.65 billion, Peter Chernin (then COO at
News Corp) claimed that 60 percent to 70 percent of YouTube traffic came
from MySpace.[6] This statistic was debated and almost certainly inflated by
Peter, but demonstrates how important MySpace was to YouTube's early
engagement.

It wasn't just a serendipitous driver engagement, but was clearly a focus
of the team's product development. While we don't have access to the product backlog from early in YouTube's development, we can look at the different product announcements the company issued. In the first five months
of maintaining a blog the company did ten blog posts, each of which highlighted between one and six new features (with the exception of the post
announcing Sequioa Capital's initial $3.5 million investment in the com-
pany). In each of the posts highlighting features, at least one of the features
was specifically about making it easier to share YouTube content—in two of
these posts this was the only feature discussed.[7]

While today this drafting strategy may look obvious, keep in mind that
YouTube still had to pay infrastructure costs to stream all those videos, even
when played on a third-party website. For context, infrastructure costs were
approximately $8 million of the $11.5 million spent from the time YouTube
was started until the time it was sold to Google, according to an analysis by
GigaOM based on the public filings in the lawsuit between YouTube and
Viacom. In that same analysis, GigaOM points out that in the last quarter

before the sale to Google these infrastructure costs scaled to over $1 million per month.[8]

Is This Strategy Defensible?

Interestingly, in both cases above, MySpace and eBay launched competing offerings. However, once YouTube and PayPal had activated and engaged these customers, it was impossible to pull them back into the core platform for video or payments. In the first chapter, when talking about the unvalidated hypotheses of our research, we discussed the myth of the first-mover advantage, but for businesses like this, I would say there *is* a "first to scale" advantage that does provide some barriers to entry. To illustrate the point, when PayPal was sold to eBay, roughly two-thirds of all PayPal payment transactions were going through eBay.[9]

In the case of MySpace and YouTube, the transformation was even more dramatic. Not only did YouTube surpass MySpace's video offering, but in August of 2006 the total number of Internet visitors to YouTube surpassed that of MySpace.[10]

While YouTube was very focused on drafting off of MySpace, rival video-sharing website Revver didn't completely ignore the social network. It's just that MySpace ultimately blocked Revver because the company wouldn't operate within MySpace's terms of service. Specifically, MySpace would not allow third-party services to run ads through its services. In other words, a video player like Revver couldn't show a short advertisement before a video if embedded on MySpace. Therefore, MySpace shut Revver's widget down. This continued to be a point of frustration right through Revver's 2008 acquisition by LiveUniverse at an inadequate price. In the announcement of the bargain-basement sale, Revver explained the reasons behind its lackluster performance in a post:

> As 2007 began, Revver was beginning to show the growth trajectory that would have allowed the company to be profitable in the not too distant future. Suddenly in mid-January 2007, Revver's proprietary video player that allowed users to post their videos on MySpace and other social

networks, stopped working on MySpace. To the average user, it appeared as if Revver's video embed was broken. Many users never understood what happened and simply thought Revver's product was poorly designed and most migrated over to services like YouTube. A smaller group of original content creator pioneers and Revver users realized the truth: that MySpace had become a predator aggressively blocking and censoring any web service it deemed competitive or that it saw generating revenue from users of the MySpace service.[11]

This is an important point: You need to operate within the constraints of the platform you are leveraging. The most obvious example of this is probably all the startups built on top of the Twitter Application Programming Interface (API) from 2007 to 2012. The experience of Twitter makes the "Is this strategy defensible?" a fair question.

If you aren't familiar with the backstory, I did an interview with Twitter co-founder Biz Stone in 2007 in which he talked about the importance of having API developers on top of the platform:

> The API has been arguably the most important, or maybe even inarguably, the most important thing we've done with Twitter. It has allowed us, first of all, to keep the service very simple and create a simple API so that developers can build on top of our infrastructure and come up with ideas that are way better than our ideas, and build things like Twitterrific, which is just a beautiful elegant way to use Twitter that we wouldn't have been able to get to, being a very small team. So, the API which has easily 10 times more traffic than the website, has been really very important to us . . .[12]

Entrepreneurial developers and startups continued to leverage the API to build on top of the Twitter platform. However, just a few years later, Twitter changed the terms of its API, which drew strong criticism and ultimately put a lot of these apps in very challenging situations. For example, *Mashable* described the change as *"squeezing the knot around the neck of third-party Twitter apps . . ."*[13]

Reflecting on the differences between Twitter, MySpace, and eBay, I've come to believe that the key to defending this platform-drafting strategy is to deliver value, even outside the platform you're drafting off of.

Airbnb performed what is perhaps one of the greatest uses of the idea of drafting off other platforms in order to drive traffic to their site. While Airbnb's early survival was pure hustle on the part of the company's founders, its later growth required some creative use of platforms such as craigslist.

Airbnb recognized that when people searched for or wanted to post a short-term rental listing, the site they used was craigslist. So Airbnb ran a campaign[14] in which they sent a message to anyone listing a place for rent on craigslist. The message would tell the listers that they could post on Airbnb, one of the largest vacation rental marketplaces on the web.[15] By understanding what their customers were searching for, Airbnb was able to identify a channel in which they could find potential customers and then go out and acquire customers in it.

B2B EXAMPLE: HUBSPOT

It'd be easy to think of this technique as restricted to business to consumer (B2C) startups given how many of the examples are consumer networks. However, the concept of finding engaged potential customers who are frustrated can work in business to business (B2B) situations as well.

While not one of the companies explicitly studied, it's hard to think of a better contemporary example than HubSpot and the techniques it has used to work on activating a channel of advertising agencies. The co-founder and CEO of HubSpot, Brian Halligan, explained to *Inc.* magazine the incredibly effective process the company used to work with this as a channel:

> In 2008, one of our sales reps came to me with an idea that he believed could revolutionize HubSpot. At the time, we sold our software directly to consumers. But the rep, Pete Caputa, thought HubSpot should have a reseller channel in order to expand the business model. Basically, he wanted to sell our core product to third parties, who would then turn around and sell the product to their customers.[16]

Pete worked on validating the idea at night and on the weekend; until, ultimately, he was "fired" from his day job as a sales rep in order to create a group within HubSpot focused on this channel program. It's been incredibly successful—in a recent interview Pete explained that the program "*produced approximately 42 percent of our customers as of June 30, 2014 and 33 percent of our revenue for the six months ended June 30, 2014.*"[17]

BUSINESS DEVELOPMENT 2.0

Coming back to the original question at the top of this chapter: How should a startup think about business development?

Caterina Fake, at the time a founder of the photo-sharing site Flickr, coined a term a few years ago, "Biz Dev 2.0," which she described as validating synergies (typically through APIs) before striking formal partnerships as opposed to starting with a formal partnership pitch and no data. As noted earlier, API is an acronym that stands for an application program interface that allows two software programs to interact with each other programatically.

The interesting thing is, over the last decade more and more companies have provided *open* APIs that allow other software applications to interact with their data and processes via these APIs. For example, a mobile developer often will use Google Maps' API to show locations of interest to users of its app (for example restaurants, coffee shops, or other local businesses) on a Google Maps interface without the customer leaving the mobile developer's app.

Coming back to Biz Dev 2.0, if you believe potential customers may be spending time frustrated on another platform and you have an API available, this is often a great approach to validating or invalidating the scalability of those communities.

If your solution is not a software product, you may not have the opportunity to start with a lightweight API-driven integration. However, you can still look for simple ways to start a conversation about partnering with an existing API before formalizing everything. For example, one of the companies I'm an investor in couldn't start with an API integration but began a critical partnership with a strategic large company in its market by doing educational webinars together and then sharing leads before formalizing a deep integrated product offering.

Most successful marriages don't start with a proposal on the first date. In the same way, most successful business partnerships don't begin with a detailed operating agreement that contemplates a lifetime together but instead start with a few simpler interactions.

PUTTING THIS INTO ACTION

Question 1: Where are the "edge cases" or small communities of your customers on other platforms?

Before you begin to draft off these platforms, realize that typically only a very small percentage of your customers will leverage your product or service on a third-party platform. Therefore, you need to analyze customer growth across all your inbound sources down to even some of the smaller ones.

The important thing to analyze is not the absolute number of individual customers coming in from that community, but a few other key variables:

- The *growth rate* of customers coming in through that channel.
- The *size* of the total audience in that channel.
- The *value* customers within that channel are getting from your product or service.

The growth rate is important, because if individuals within another platform start to realize you are the solution to the problem they are experiencing, they should be making others aware of the solution with no marketing necessary on your part. You will later optimize these referrals through the next step of this process, but there should already be organic growth at a rapid pace on a percentage basis, even if small in absolute numbers.

As in Chapter 3, where you estimated the total market for your product or service, you want to also ask yourself how large the total audience is within the channel you are considering. The goal here is to avoid optimizing for a platform that ultimately won't deliver a meaningful number of customers to your product. Again, as in Chapter 3, it's important to investigate the growth rate of your potential partner.

Finally, you want to make sure that your customers are getting real value from your products or services within the platform you're investigating. Some of the same techniques you used in Chapter 4 to investigate the value of your solution can now be used to investigate the same thing but focused explicitly on customers arriving via that platform.

Question 2: What can you do to make it easier to use your product on the chosen platforms?

Once you've identified a promising platform to draft off of, the next step is to take friction out of the process of using your product or service on that platform. Similar to the discussion in Chapter 5, you want to reduce all friction involved in customers using your product on these third-party platforms.

Earlier in this chapter, we talked about a number of product design and development techniques that the companies above used to make this reduction of friction easier. However, don't overlook some of the simpler approaches as well, like simply writing helpful support documentation or tutorials to make it easier for the customer to get started. Remember from earlier in this chapter that most of YouTube's early blog posts were focused specifically on emphasizing product integrations, and many included direct links to support documentation.

Question 3: Longer term, what can you do to formalize the partnership once traction has been demonstrated?

The emphasis on starting with simple integrations instead of complex negotiations doesn't eliminate the importance of following up and having face-to-face partnership discussions once the value between your solution and the partner platform has been demonstrated.

It's important that you end up with a formal business relationship as your solution starts to become meaningful to both you and your partner.

How to best structure that depends on the particular engagement, but don't hesitate to get creative.

In fact, you often need to get a little creative to get the right relationship structured. As PayPal became the dominant payment platform for eBay transactions, the relationship between the companies was very tense. PayPal convinced eBay to allow it to exhibit at a convention being organized in June of 2002. PayPal sent 30 people to the show and handed out as many T-shirts as possible. Peter Thiel credits eBay seeing so many of their key merchants wearing PayPal T-shirts as part of what changed the trajectory of the conversation, ultimately resulting in eBay's acquisition of PayPal.[18]

8

OPTIMIZING ALGORITHMS

"Software is eating the world."

—Marc Andreesen[1]

IF YOU TAKE A LOOK AROUND, YOU'LL REALIZE THAT MOST OF OUR DAY-to-day lives run on software. Computers assist in everything from helping cities to reduce traffic by optimizing the timing of traffic lights to finding the best price on a flight or hotel and then providing intelligent predictions based on historical information on whether a consumer should buy now or wait. Software-enabled startups have also transformed entire markets, from the taxi industry being disrupted by Uber to hotels facing similar disruption from Airbnb.

When you consider that 64 percent of Americans carry around in their pocket a computer (smartphone) that is more powerful than a desktop computer was only a few years ago, it's clear most of our daily activity likely involves some level of interaction with software.[2]

While the ubiquity of software is an important trend in general, the critical element discussed in this chapter is the increasing number of purchasing decisions that are being automated by software algorithms. The term "algorithm"—formerly used only in computer science and math—crept into the public's vocabulary, only becoming a broadly used term after the now-famous Netflix challenge.

The idea was that Netflix provided anonymous information on the rental history of different customers along with their ratings of those rentals. The company challenged teams of engineers to come up with a better algorithm that would provide Netflix customers with more accurate recommendations of films they might enjoy.

The contest was covered by major media outlets including *Wired* magazine, the *Wall Street Journal,* and the *New York Times* and was also discussed later in at least two *New York Times* best-selling business books—*Wikinomics* and *Freakonomics.* Suddenly everyone seemed to have at least a cursory understanding of computer algorithms.

As a reminder, Netflix uses these algorithms to present personalized movie recommendations to you based on your previous viewing and rating behavior. For example, one customer may have recently watched and rated eight movies. Perhaps four of the eight could be categorized under the genre "romantic comedy" while the other four movies could all fall into the "action" genre. When looking at the ratings, it might become obvious that the person watching these movies prefers action films, as those films all received four- and five-star ratings, while the romantic comedies each received just one star. Based on these ratings, it is straightforward to infer the person watching and rating these movies prefers action movies. However, there are obviously too many action movies for that to be enough information to present a list of the films this particular viewer would most enjoy.

Therefore, the algorithm also takes into consideration more details about the films, such as who the lead actor is. While getting closer, that still isn't enough detail on an individual's preferences to sort results. So Netflix and other similar services use a technique called collaborative filtering, in which they look at how other customers in their database rated similar movies and look for movies you may not yet have watched that other people with similar preferences have enjoyed. Even if you've never experienced this on Netflix, you probably have seen collaborative filtering at work on Amazon when they recommend products to you based on what other people like you have purchased.

While the approach is conceptually straightforward, in practice it is very difficult to do for millions of customers. That's why, in 2006, Netflix launched a challenge to see if any teams of computer scientists could come up with an algorithm that was at least 10 percent better than the recommendations provided by their current recommendation algorithm. In return, they would pay that team a $1 million prize.

In just the first year of the contest, over 20,000 teams tried it, and over 2,000 of those teams actually submitted an entry.[3] At the end of that first year, no one had achieved the target of a 10 percent improvement, so the company paid out a $50,000 progress prize to the team in the lead and resumed the competition. Ultimately, a seven-person team won the prize in September of 2009 after more than 5,600 different teams had entered proposed improvements over the three years.[4]

One interesting anecdote many people don't know: Netflix never fully deployed the algorithm that won the contest. While the prize-winner certainly performed better in the lab, Netflix explained that the "focus on improving Netflix personalization had shifted to the next level by then." They would go on to describe a number of ways that their focus had shifted, including, "We have discovered through the years that there is tremendous value to our subscribers in incorporating recommendations to personalize as much of Netflix as possible."[5] In other words, they have shifted focus from using algorithms to drive *one* list of movie predictions to incorporating these algorithms *across* the service.

Now let me tell you why I am going to all the trouble of explaining what an algorithm is. Of the companies we studied, it's become clear that many of those that went into business most recently were able to leverage understanding of an algorithm's underlying software to increase their likelihood of being discovered by potential customers. This is more than simply trusting an algorithm to make the best recommendation; instead entrepreneurs are actively trying to "game" the results by optimizing elements of their solution to deliver disproportionate awareness of their solution relative to competitors.

Sometimes a consumer inputs keywords into a text box and then the *search algorithm* finds the "best" results based on the keywords entered. The most common examples of this would be search results in Google or Amazon. More recently, these recommendations were completely automated based on an individual's prior behavior and/or simply a measure of popularity. Examples of popularity-based recommendations include everything from "app store" recommendations to social news aggregators like Digg or Reddit.

The mathematical rules used to prioritize the results are called computer algorithms. At their simplest level, they are just a set of instructions written in computer language that create relevant output based on inputs. Per above, those inputs can be explicit information such as a keyword the user enters or more implicit behavior such as items that a customer and similar customers have viewed or purchased in the past.

EVERYONE NEEDS TO CARE ABOUT ALGORITHMS

We will walk through some more examples in a moment. However, some of you may be feeling like this is advice restricted to software companies. I believe this is a technique that all businesses need to keep in mind. The way algorithms rank results are impacting local businesses like restaurants, bars, and coffee shops. For example, if you own a Japanese restaurant in Atlanta, you want to do everything you can to figure out how to get your restaurant to come up first on Google when a potential customer searches for "japanese food near atlanta."

Since most consumers only look at the first few search results, the difference in a few spots can be significant. A recent study by online ad network Chitika showed that 32.5 percent of search traffic goes to the business in the top position on Google and over 60 percent of the traffic goes to the top three positions.[6]

You can see how important the results from Google's search algorithm are to our fictitious restaurant or to any business. It's not just search results though. Mobile solutions like Yelp are increasingly becoming a popular way to discover local businesses. A few years ago, Harvard Business School Professor Michael Luca set out to try and quantify the impact of an increase in the average star ratings of a restaurant. He gathered data for every restaurant in Seattle, Washington, from 2003 to 2009, looking specifically at their Yelp reviews and revenues. After analyzing the results he concluded:

> . . . a one-star increase on Yelp leads to a 5 to 9 percent increase in revenue. Yet Yelp doesn't work for all restaurants. Chain restaurants—which

already spend heavily on branding—are unaffected by changes in their Yelp ratings. This suggests that consumer reviews present a new way of learning in the Internet age, and are fast becoming a substitute for traditional forms of reputation.[7]

In other words, if you have millions of dollars to spend on brand advertising, you may not have to worry as much about reviews. However, if you don't have that budget or want to spend your money more wisely, getting reviews to game the Yelp recommendation algorithms can be a great way to leapfrog the branding process as a local restaurant.

While the owner of our fictitious Japanese restaurant in Atlanta may not know the results of Professor Luca's research, it's increasingly obvious to her that a positive Yelp review can help the restaurant earn money and make it easier for potential customers to locate. Based on this, she may proudly display "People Love Us on Yelp" stickers to try and get more customers to impact the algorithm's rankings by providing five-star reviews. These stickers are a great example of the actions small business owners can take in order to help themselves become more favored by recommendation algorithms.

I wonder how many restaurant or coffee shop owners five years ago thought they'd have to worry about optimizing software algorithm results? I'd argue, very few. Today, the difference between a good Yelp score and a poor one can mean the difference between a thriving business and one on life support.

While there are great examples of how to use algorithms to a company's advantage in many of the recently started companies we studied, none may have been better at this technique than Mint. This is probably not surprising given that optimizing algorithms is a relatively new trend and given that the founder had experience working on algorithms before starting Mint.

MINT

As a reminder, Mint grew to 1.5 million users in just two years, and was then sold to Intuit for $170 million. Mint did this in a market in which it had numerous competitors, some of which were being backed by large banks with deep pockets or by other premier VCs, including Wesabe, which was founded almost a year earlier.

Mint was also operating in a market that most people don't like to talk about—personal finance. In order to compete in this crowded and challenging market, Mint got creative with its marketing efforts and was able to leverage three different recommendation algorithms to drive awareness and customers: Google search results, social news aggregators, and the iTunes App Store. In each case, Mint strategically optimized its strategies to work with each service's underlying algorithm.

Mint's Google Strategy

When figuring out how to optimize its Google results, Mint realized that people were not going to Google to search for "personal finance software." Rather, Mint determined that people were more likely to be using terms that approximated their problems, such as "money help." As Figure 8.1 quantifies, according to Google Trends people are, in fact, almost four times as likely to search for the latter.[8]

Mint created a blog of financial advice long before it had even completed its budget software. As people searched for this information, they discovered useful content about budgeting and personal articles written by the team at Mint designed to inspire readers to get their finances in order. These articles were helpful to the customer, but also great sources of leads for Mint's service.

It's worth taking a moment to point out that these articles were truly useful. While Mint took steps to write articles about topics its customers were searching for, the company also made sure the articles were helpful in answering the visitor's questions, whether the visitor ultimately became a Mint customer or not.

As people have studied the process of optimizing a website's visibility, there has been a division between so-called white hat and black hat search engine optimization techniques. The idea is that there is a group of techniques (black hat) in which you try to mislead the search engine about how

Figure 8.1—Google Search Term Comparison

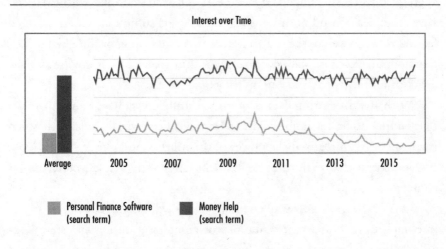

relevant your content is in order to capture user traffic, users who will ultimately be disappointed with the content they discover. Companies like Google have been working very hard over the last number of years to stop the effectiveness of these techniques. Ignoring the ethics of many of these approaches, I'd just point out that in many cases small changes to the algorithm have ended up destroying the effectiveness of these techniques overnight, making it a very suspect and brittle strategy in my opinion.

Then there is behavior like Mint engaged in, described above. In that case, the company is simply trying to make sure its relevant content is as discoverable as possible. This is called white hat optimization and something in which anyone who believes search is a key part of their business should invest.

Social Aggregation

Mint's blog went on to become the number one personal finance blog online.[9] As Mint's former lead designer, Jason Putorti, told website analytics provider KISS Metrics, "Our app didn't have a high viral coefficient, but we had content that [did]."[10]

In fact, the Mint content was so viral it was even shared on social news aggregation sites like Digg and Reddit. If you aren't familiar with these services, the idea behind both websites is that users submit articles discovered from across the web to the site and other users then vote for the articles. The most popular content, based an an algorithm that looks at how recent the article is and its votes, ends up on the home page.

With Reddit getting over 170 million unique visitors a month,[11] an article ending up on the home page can be a significant driver of traffic. When the team at Mint realized the power of this traffic source they started looking at content that performed well on these sites and created more similar content.

One of the most powerful content types for these sites is what are called infographics or visual representations of complex information. Stew Langille, Mint's director of marketing through its acquisition by Intuit, realized that this kind of content actually resulted in 30 times as much traffic as comparable articles just written as text. He was so convinced that infographics are the best way to win customers that he became co-founder and CEO of Visual.ly, a company specifically focused on infographic-style content, after leaving Intuit.[12]

Pre-Marketing

As noted, Mint actually started its blog before the service even launched. The company was able to leverage the blog's popularity into a list of over 20,000 individuals who wanted to be beta testers of Mint's web app. The demand was so great that Mint's system couldn't initially handle all 20,000. So Mint again got creative, and urged those who wanted early access to Mint to post an "I want Mint" badge on their blog or social media profile, which helped boost the rankings for Mint's blog content even further (because one of the most important measures of relevancy for Google is the number of "inbound links" or websites that link to your site) and generated even more buzz for the young company as prospective new customers discovered the service by visiting fans' pages on which the badge advertising was displayed.[13]

Those who posted the badge were then given preference for early beta testing of Mint.com. All of this content creation was so successful that by the time Mint launched its service, it had more traffic than the combined traffic of all other personal finance websites.[14]

Mint iPhone App

It's also important to make sure you continue to examine upcoming platforms that can be significant customer drivers and note how individuals discover products on that platform. For example, Mint was originally a web-based service only. Yet in the middle of 2008, about a year after the iPhone was launched, the company started exploring a mobile strategy.

Aaron Forth, Mint's vice president of product, explained at the time that it was not an obvious choice given all of its revenue was based on individuals visiting Mint.com. However, a few years later 20 percent of its customers rely exclusively on accessing the service via mobile phone and most have linked their accounts to a mobile phone.

When Mint decided to launch, it focused originally on the iOS platform exclusively, given resource constraints. (The company would later launch an Android app less than a year after being acquired by Intuit.)[15]

In a presentation at SxSW, Aaron explained that their goal up front was to be a top three app in the free finance category—understanding that being at the top of the list is critical to success, just as it is for the Google search results described earlier. Mint succeeded in creating one of the most popular apps, which did indeed drive significant new account creation. By 2011, 20 percent of signups were originating from mobile apps, and most customers had linked their mobile phones to their Mint accounts.[16]

This leads to an important point about this process: You always need to be looking for the *next* algorithm that is coming along and providing distribution. In most cases, there are opportunities to drive a breakthrough growth strategy if you get to a platform and start optimizing the process before "everyone" knows about it. For example, today the process of trying to optimize Google search results is much more difficult than it was a few years ago. However, today there are new platforms that look more like the early days of search engine optimization.

AIRBNB

Mint is a great case study on how to use different recommendation algorithms to your advantage by creating value for your customers through content that goes beyond just selling your product, but there are numerous other examples out there. Another recent success story from our research is Airbnb.

After spending ten years at eBay coordinating its search engine optimization (SEO) efforts, Dennis Goedegebuure joined Airbnb in a similar role. He explained to *Inc.* magazine that as the individual responsible for ensuring good search results, his role focused on "technical implementations of daily search engine optimization, and about long-term strategy including content projects."[17]

One of these long-term content projects revolved around the 25th anniversary of the Berlin Wall coming down. The impetus for the project was an email the company received in May of 2012 from a guest, Catherine, about an experience she had with her father, Jorg, who had used Airbnb to stay in Berlin.

Dennis explained:

> Jorg had been a border guard on the West German side of the border during the Cold War, but moved to Denmark before German reunification. He never had closure on his experience as a guard, and had many barriers in his head towards Germany. At their Airbnb in Berlin they met Kai, who had also been a border guard, but on the East side of the Wall. Meeting Kai and hearing that he had such similar experiences helped Jorg overcome his demons towards Germany and break down the barriers and preconceptions in his mind.[18]

As the 25th anniversary approached, Dennis's group at Airbnb created a YouTube video about the story and within four days of launching the video on the service, it already had two million views. Today the video has had over 5.8 million views. This was the anchor of a larger campaign around the 25th anniversary. Airbnb also did events, created a microsite with the film and interview, and purchased TV advertising.[19]

LINKEDIN

Most people have probably gone to Google when searching to find out information about someone they were about to meet for the first time or trying to remember how they know someone. LinkedIn decided to optimize their members' profile pages to show up high in those search results to drive awareness of the service.

In February 2006, about three years after launching LinkedIn, the company started leveraging this behavior by creating a new feature called "public profiles" which simply allowed members to show a version of their LinkedIn profile to everyone, including people they weren't connected with. A history of the company on the LinkedIn website states: "With the launch of public profiles, LinkedIn begins to stake its claim as the professional profile of record."[20]

This is certainly true, but making profiles public also served to build awareness of the service with individuals who first discovered LinkedIn when looking at someone else's profile. It's also worth pointing out that because LinkedIn waited to launch public profiles until it had a few million members, public profiles immediately became highly ranked pages when searches were conducted.

CAUTIONARY TALE: SPOKE

Spoke tried to take a similar approach, but did so earlier in its development by crawling and extracting information to populate people's profiles without getting their consent. While it was a great technique to build awareness, unfortunately it was not the type of awareness Spoke was hoping for.

This approach resulted in many inaccurate profile pages and also made some people concerned about the privacy implications of what Spoke was doing. This in turn resulted in negative reviews[21] and concerns about violation of individuals' privacy.[22] Spoke should have focused on the prerequisites—specifically creating an excellent first interaction—like LinkedIn, before exploring techniques to draft off platforms.

PUTTING THIS INTO ACTION

Question 1: What are the sources driving awareness today?

Understand the algorithms that will affect you the most and then seek to understand the rules behind those algorithms. Or put another way, figure out how your product is finding customers today.

Perhaps you're the proprietor of a restaurant. Well then, you'll probably want to spend your time learning about Yelp and how it can affect your business and what actions you can take to leverage Yelp. Or maybe you're a new startup, trying to drive awareness. Understanding how social aggregators like Hacker News, Digg, and Reddit can help people discover your product would be a great starting point.

The point is, think about where a customer might just come across your product, even if they didn't search for it, and then think about how you can make sure the probability of customers just stumbling across your product is as high as it can possibly be. To do this you'll want to study the recommendation platforms or algorithms most pertinent to you. Also, as we saw in the discussion on Mint's iPhone app, don't forget to pay special attention to emerging platforms.

Question 2: How would you deconstruct these algorithms?

This can be difficult, as most companies don't publish all the details of their algorithm publicly, to avoid spammers using black hat techniques to destroy the relevancy of the results.

However, for almost any popular recommendation system there are typically blog posts and experts who can provide some insights into how the systems work. The companies also typically provide some insights directly, which can be useful clues even if not the whole picture.

For example, in the case of Google, there are numerous conferences, books, and blogs that cover in detail how the algorithm works as well as any expected changes. While Google will typically make 500 or 600 changes a year to its algorithm, the company does major changes a few times a year. Usually, Google releases at least a partial preview of these changes, which are analyzed in great detail by the press, given the impact the changes have on so many businesses.

If you are having trouble getting details on how the rankings work, you also can look at what similar top-ranked businesses are doing. For example, look at Apple's App Store to see what kind of catchy titles and descriptions the top apps in your category use.

Question 3: How would you optimize your product's performance in regards to these algorithms?

Based on this newfound understanding of how the algorithms work, you can shift your attention to understanding what behavior your customers will likely engage in to discover your solution.

While the algorithms will recommend your product (and often competitive products) to prospective customers, you need to understand the behavior prompting that recommendation. For example, what keywords are they searching for? Where are they searching for you? What other type of content might they find valuable in addition to whatever you are selling?

Think about Mint or LinkedIn: They understood that their ideal potential customers would probably not be searching for personal financial management software or a professional profile page, but would probably be searching for advice related to finance or information on contacts they were about to meet. Based on this insight, the two companies took very different approaches to optimizing their discoverability. In Mint's case, the company created a ton of quality content related to personal finance that was more in line with what their potential customers were searching for and was therefore more likely to come up on the search results. In LinkedIn's case, the company actually leveraged their existing member profiles by optimizing them to show up high in search results.

Rapid iteration is key. Since you're not spending big bucks on static advertising campaigns you can experiment with a variety of techniques, from discounts for patrons who use social media to promote you through "Likes" and "tweets," to playing around with different content such as blogs, videos, newsletters, and more. The possibilities are really only limited by your creativity.

To optimize the recommendation algorithms you don't need to be a tech genius. As Mint shows, you can drive traffic through something as simple as quality writing shared on your favorite websites!

Question 4: How can you think like a publisher?

As we've seen, most recommendation algorithms are simply looking to make their users happy by recommending the best option for that user. The best way to be recommended is to have a great product—but assuming you've satisfied the prerequisites in section one of this book, that should go without saying.

A simple way to get people talking about you is to have great content that provides value to the user/customer and isn't necessarily an advertisement, but relates to the problem you are solving. A helpful exercise is to challenge yourself and your colleagues to imagine you are the editorial team of a magazine or online property geared for your potential customers. In the examples above, for example, Airbnb would be an online travel magazine and Mint would be a publisher of a personal finance site. It's helpful to think about what content those editors would create and then think how you can integrate that into your site's content strategy.

It's worth pointing out that Airbnb has recently taken this idea to the extreme: In November 2014 it launched a quarterly print magazine called *Pineapple*. The *New York Times* described the magazine:

> The 128-page winter 2014 issue, which carries no advertising, contains features on three cities popular among Airbnb hosts and guests: San Francisco, where the company is based; London; and Seoul, South Korea.
>
> In an introductory note, the magazine said it aimed "to explore our fundamental values: sharing, community and belonging," and to "inspire and motivate exploration, not just within the cities featured, but within any space a reader finds themselves."[23]

While I wouldn't recommend starting with a print magazine (remember this was launched six years after Airbnb was founded), it does reinforce how important content can be as part of a strategy. The CMO of Airbnb, Jonathan Mildenhall, explained this overall strategy when describing the Berlin Wall anniversary campaign discussed earlier in this chapter:

> Great content and storytelling is so important now for any brand . . . As a community-driven company, we don't want to just talk about our product, but instead put our community front and center of any campaign.[24]

Every brand would be well served to think how it can employ similar storytelling techniques.

9

VIRAL GROWTH

Measuring and Optimizing

"Recommendations from people we know are the most trusted form of marketing."

—Nielsen

WHEN I MOVED TO NEW YORK CITY, IT WAS TO LIVE ON AN ENTREPRE-neur's budget. In other words, I needed to keep my rent as low as possible, and as you may have heard, New York is an expensive place to live. After searching, I finally settled on an apartment on 109th Street between Broad-way and Amsterdam. I went back to that neighborhood recently and it was completely different, but at the time, although it was only a few blocks from the entrance to Columbia University, I was the only person in my building (and possibly on my block) who spoke English as a first language.

I loved the neighborhood, and armed with two six-packs of cerveza and an afternoon to lose a few dollars, I immediately befriended a group of four older Puerto Rican gentlemen who played dominos at the entrance to our building. It was a great deal, as they effectively functioned as doormen for the apartment building during my entire stay there and spent the next two years looking out for me.

A few times a week, one of them would pull me aside and tell me about a few new products he'd recently discovered. Everything from a good new beer to a new taco stand to some electronic product his son had given him. He was quick to refer these products to me, and I often took him up on his recommendations.

This gets to the main point of this chapter.

Your current customers can be one of your most significant growth engines as you scale an innovative product or service.

More importantly, this isn't a new phenomenon. Customers have been a great source of referrals long before Mark Zuckerberg was even born. However,

Figure 9.1 Measuring Referral Impact

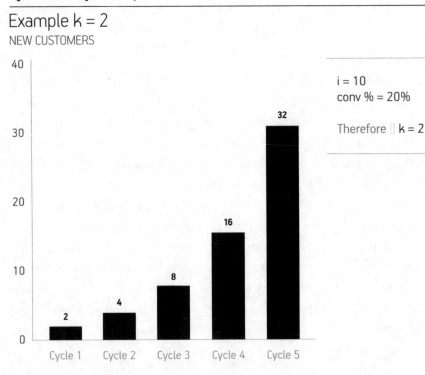

Example k = 2
NEW CUSTOMERS

i = 10
conv % = 20%

Therefore ‖ k = 2

the fact that our lives are becoming increasingly connected digitally creates the possibility for:

- Reducing the friction at the point when a customer is most likely to make a referral
- Measure the effectiveness of different interactions to increase sharing

MATH

To the second point, the math is actually very straightforward but worth reviewing quickly.

The mathematical model for measuring how effective your product or service is at winning referrals is often described as your viral coefficient.

Most of the writing I've seen on this focuses on the use of a simple calculation model in which the number of invitations a new customer sends out (typically represented by the variable i) is multiplied by the conversion rate of those invitations (conv %).

The viral coefficient is typically calculated as k, so the formula is:

$$k = i * \text{conv } \%$$

When k results in a value greater than 1, you have achieved a product that can organically grow virally. In other words, for every customer you add that customer will in turn bring in at least one more customer.

This leads to the obvious question: What is a good viral coefficient? The answer, as unsatisfactory as it may feel, is that it really depends.

For certain products—those for which you need to build a large set of engaged customers without paid customer acquisition—your viral coefficient must be significantly greater than 1. The idea is that with a viral coefficient greater than 1, for every customer who signs up you will add at least one more customer. This will result in perpetual growth.

In other cases, a viral coefficient of even 0.5 may be fine, as you can supplement that with paid customer acquisition techniques—either marketing or sales—and leverage the referrals simply as a way to drive down your cost of customer acquisition.

In any case, it's helpful to track your viral coefficient across time by cohort and work on iterations to optimize it.

SLIGHTLY MORE SOPHISTICATED MODEL

As David Skok (a fellow serial-entrepreneur-turned-VC) points out on his blog,[1] the simple mathematical model discussed above is limited in one important aspect: It doesn't take into consideration how quickly new customers send out additional invitations. To remedy this omission, David introduces a new variable: cycle time (*ct*). The impact of *ct* on *k* is dramatic—specifically it increases *k* at any point in time (*t*) to the power of *t/ct*.

Going back to our first example, let's look at how changing the cycle time between 5, 10, 15, and 20 days will affect growth of a service with a viral coefficient of 2.

As you can see, the impact of reducing cycle time is dramatic. Forty days out the difference between a cycle time of 5 and 10 is 511 vs 31. The delta will continue to expand over time.

Figure 9.2—Impact of Reducing Cycle Time

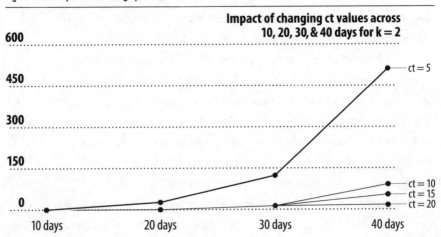

TECHNIQUES TO CONSIDER

Given this model, the key question then is: *How do you decrease cycle time* (ct) *and increase the number of invitations sent* (i) *and conversion rate?*

I'd argue that the key to improving the conversion rate is continuing to iterate on the importance of a great first interaction. However, you need to make sure you're using the data to optimize this rate without getting stuck at a local maxima (we'll discuss data in more detail in the next chapter).

As we reviewed the case studies in our research, a few techniques for increasing invites sent (*i*) and decreasing cycle time (*ct*) emerged.

1. Look for content for non-users created by users and make it easy to share

As discussed in Chapter 7, in many ways an early catalyst for YouTube's growth was its ability to draft off of MySpace. Although, certainly, the first key insight was that MySpace page authors wanted the ability to put You-Tube videos on their site. The next part of this, and relating directly to the focus of this chapter, was to make it very easy for other MySpace authors—visiting a connection that had already posted a YouTube video—to realize that they could do the same thing.

While MySpace is much less popular today, the principle is still being applied on a variety of social platforms. As Figure 9.3 shows, at the bottom of every YouTube video is the option to share it on 13 different third-party platforms with a single click.

Figure 9.3—YouTube Sharing Options

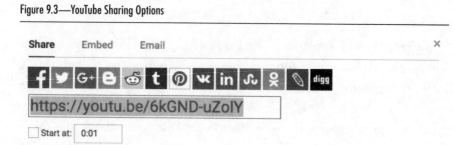

Hotmail applied a variation on this principle, adding a note to the bottom of every email being sent out. Below the signature by default, Hotmail included a message explaining the email had been sent from a Hotmail account and provided a link for the recipient to sign up for their own free account.

This was an incredibly successful technique and led to Hotmail becoming one of the first examples of "viral growth" in an Internet company. Early investor Steve Jurvetson actually wrote an article on his venture firm's website, explaining the power of this marketing technique. He explained that Hotmail included

> . . . a promotional pitch for its Web-based email with a clickable URL in every outbound message sent by a Hotmail user. Therein lay one of the critical elements of viral marketing: every customer becomes an involuntary salesperson simply by using the product.[2]

Steve went on to contrast Hotmail's techniques with those used by competitor Juno (both companies were analyzed in our research), comparing the marketing budgets of Hotmail and Juno and explaining that Hotmail achieved 12 million users of the service in 18 months with a marketing budget of $50,000, while Juno's $20 million marketing budget for traditional advertisements delivered significantly fewer customers.[3]

The growth Hotmail produced at the time was unprecedented, and the company was arguably the first great example of how much easier it is for a product to spread virally given the reduction in friction made possible by the use of Internet products.

2. Incentivize users with money or rewards

In the early days of its platform, PayPal famously paid both the friend who referred the new customer and the customer who signed up $10. While this led to some gaming of the system (people creating multiple email addresses and signing themselves up to profit $20 per account), it did catalyze the company's early growth, as co-founder Peter Thiel talks about in *Zero to One*:

At PayPal, our initial user base was 24 people, all of whom worked at Pay-Pal. Acquiring customers through banner advertising proved too expensive. However, by directly paying people to sign up and then paying them more to refer friends, we achieved extraordinary growth. This strategy cost us $20 per customer, but it also led to 7% daily growth, which meant that our user base nearly doubled every 10 days. After four or five months, we had hundreds of thousands of users and a viable opportunity to build a great company by servicing money transfers for small fees that ended up greatly exceeding our customer acquisition cost.[4]

A more recent example of using rewards to incentivize users would be Dropbox. Founder and CEO Drew Houston gave a presentation in 2010 in which he credits the PayPal referral program for inspiring the word-of-mouth marketing technique that ultimately drove Dropbox's viral growth. As a backdrop, after launching in September of 2008 the company tried many traditional marketing techniques to gain customers, including doing PR and buying cost-per-click advertising on Google. Unfortunately, as Drew explained, the cost of acquiring customers was between $233 and $388 for a $99 product, which obviously was not sustainable. However, Dropbox's core customers did love the product and were telling their friends about it. This was key to the company's "epiphany" 14 months after launch, when it decided to focus on optimizing its growth by providing incentives—in the form of additional free storage—to both the person sharing files and to the person receiving the shared files, if they signed up. This new, optimized referral program increased signups by 60 percent and has led to "sustained 15–20 percent month-over-month growth" since the program was rolled out.[5]

3. Optimize for your best customers

It's easy to be misled by looking at the averages across all your customers using either of the mathematical models for viral coefficients described above. However, you often need to look at calculations and make optimizations for specific segments. For example, typically your most engaged customers are those who drive the most referrals. Given this, sometimes you do need to introduce features to optimize for your power users without complicating the first early interaction (Chapter 5).

There are lots of examples of how to do this, but my personal favorite is the arrival of Facebook's News Feed. While Facebook has made regular tweaks to the interaction since originally launching in September of 2006, it was this seminal change that introduced the reverse-chronological "feed" of updates to the people you were connected with on Facebook. While this feature had been used previously by services like RSS readers that allowed users to subscribe to new content published by blogs and other media sites, Facebook's News Feed was arguably the advent of what has become the standard interaction paradigm for social network updates.

Unfortunately for Facebook, at the time this was not how the roughly eight million students who used the site regularly expected to interact with the platform. Many of them quickly decided to let Facebook know they weren't happy about it, creating groups on Facebook to protest. A *Time* magazine article that came out the week the changes were made described what followed:

> Since Tuesday (the first day of the new feature), a handful of anti-News Feed groups have sprung up on Facebook. The largest has 284,000 members and is called "Students Against Facebook News Feed (Official Petition to Facebook)." The group was created yesterday morning by Ben Parr,[6] a junior at Northwestern University, who was disgusted to find the News Feed when he logged into Facebook. With a meeting to get to, Parr quickly created a group, told a few friends about it and left his computer. When he came back a few hours later, the membership was at 13,000 and the numbers climbed steadily throughout the day, reaching 100,000 at 2 a.m.—at which point Parr called it a night.[7]

What is interesting is that this quick growth of membership within a Facebook group, with no advertising and minimal promotion, demonstrated precisely how effective the new "feed-based" way of interacting with Facebook was. Instead of having to search around Ben's profile looking for the group he had created, everyone who joined the group could immediately broadcast that to their friends' feed. This had to reassure the team at Facebook they were on the right path with this new user interface paradigm.

4. Leverage existing connections

It's easy to overlook the reality that at some point, you just need to make it easier for people to remember who they'd want to invite. As we mapped connections across digital services like Facebook and Twitter, we have found this simple point to be particularly true.

In 2004, fewer than one out of every four new LinkedIn users actually went through the process of typing in email addresses and inviting new users into the social network. This obviously constrained the growth of the network significantly. So the LinkedIn team created an Outlook plug-in that automatically examined a new user's contacts for potential invites. The feature was extremely popular with 7 percent of all new users who took advantage of this functionality and it increased the number of invitations sent by new users by 30 percent.

It's easy to think about platforms of social connections such as LinkedIn, Facebook, and Twitter—but this is a good reminder that we also have plenty of social connections via slightly less obvious digital repositories like our email or cell phone address books.

PUTTING THIS INTO ACTION

Question 1: How can you "gamify" the act of getting your customers to refer you to other customers?

A term that has gained popularity in the last few years is "gamification," which *Webster's Dictionary* defines as: "The process of adding games or gamelike elements to something (as a task) so as to encourage participation."[8]

Companies have been trying to use incentives to get people to take certain actions for a long time, using techniques like giving customers stamps, which could later be redeemed for free prizes or discounted services, with each purchase. However, at the beginning of this decade offering some kind of incentive became a standard recommendation from most management consultants. In fact, one of the large analysis firms actually published a report stating that "70% of Global 2000 companies will have at least one gamified application."[9]

While the strategy certainly can be forced, I do think it's helpful to think about the incentives you can use to get your customers to do other activities, and specifically, in the context of this chapter, get them to refer your business to their connections who then become customers.

One of the best examples of this from our study—an incentive method most professionals have experienced—comes again from LinkedIn. The company has done a fantastic job using different techniques over the years to get individuals to fill out information on their profile. As you may recall, for a long time the incentive was to get your profile "100% complete." The irony of this metric was obviously that the system didn't actually know what a complete professional profile for any individual user was, but many people (myself included) are motivated to complete the tasks we start, including, in this case, the task of creating a LinkedIn profile. More recently I logged in and saw LinkedIn now has a concept of "profile strength" with different rankings associated with it.

Question 2: What story does your customer interaction data tell?

The next chapter is going to discuss the role data plays in high-growth companies. Specifically, that of informing but not blindly driving key decisions. As was discussed at the beginning of this chapter, it's easier and easier to measure the key indicators that drive how effective and efficient your solution is at getting customers to refer other customers. Pay attention to this data and look for opportunities to optimize it.

Of particular importance is exploring the data on the customer's interaction with your product to understand the "wow" moment when customers really get excited about the solution you are providing. This is a point when you can really incentivize sharing, as it's easier to share when someone is getting additional utility or just generally impressed.

Question 3: If your product itself isn't viral, what can you do to create viral content about the problem you're solving?

As I have talked to business leaders about making their products and services more viral, many are quick to point out that either because of the characteristics of their target customer or the problem that they are solving, their customers are less likely to refer other companies to their product or service.

Mint is an interesting example of this. Most people don't like to talk about their personal finances (except maybe on January 1 every year, in general terms, when announcing their New Year's resolutions). The Mint team realized this was going to make it difficult for individuals using the application to share that with their friends. However, what Mint ended up understanding is that while use of the product wasn't viral, they could create content that was very viral. It's a helpful question to ask yourself: What content can I create that can go viral, even if my solution won't? In the case of Mint, as discussed last chapter, this was content based around helping with personal finances.

SECTION III

ELEMENTS FOR SUSTAINED LONG-TERM GROWTH

THE KEY TO CONSTRUCTING A TALL BUILDING IS NOT SIMPLY WHAT YOU see aboveground, but a solid foundation beneath the ground. High-growth projects are the same way—they can collapse if not supported by the right foundation.

A business can be launched into the market's consciousness by just one catalyzing event, only to be just as quickly forgotten. Once you've satisfied the four prerequisites described in section one and gotten the attention of your core advocates using one or more of the best practices in the previous section, the final step is to make sure you have a solid foundation for long-term growth.

This last section goes through five foundational elements that I believe are critical for sustained long-term high growth.

Ned Renzi, my partner at Birchmere Ventures, who was also on the board at Cvent, likes to call it the "11-year overnight success." It takes time to build a large company, even if you are growing quickly. The public will never be aware of most of the true building blocks as they are put into place. While there are techniques you can use to accelerate this growth and increase awareness, as described in the last section, the five best practices described in the following chapters are essential to ultimately sustaining your goals.

10

BE DATA INFORMED
(NOT DATA DRIVEN)

"Not everything that can be counted counts, and not everything that counts can be counted."

—Albert Einstein

THERE IS A FAMOUS STORY ABOUT INDIA WHEN IT WAS A BRITISH COLONY. The government became very concerned about poisonous cobra snakes in Delhi, so it offered a reward for every dead snake handed over. While the program was an initial success, some imaginative individuals started breeding the cobras, only to kill them and collect the bounty. When the government became aware of this, it stopped the program, prompting the breeders to release all their newly "worthless" snakes into the wild, making the cobra situation ultimately much worse.

While some historians debate the historical validity of this parable, it illustrates an important principle: Individuals will go to great lengths to optimize the metrics on which they are being compensated—so we need to collect information by measuring things that are actually important, and make sure those metrics can't be gamed.

As we've transitioned into a digital world, it's become easier and easier to generate an overwhelming amount of data about our business. Increasingly, across executive boardrooms, the conversation has revolved around this "big data" opportunity. A 2011 report by McKinsey & Company, *Big Data: The Next Frontier for Innovation, Competition, and Productivity*,[1] explained how ubiquitous this information is across industries.

> Big data has now reached every sector in the global economy. Like other essential factors of production such as hard assets and human capital, much of modern economic activity simply couldn't take place without it. We estimate that by 2009, nearly all sectors in the US economy had at least an average of 200 terabytes of stored data (twice the size of US retailer Wal-Mart's data warehouse in 1999) per company with more than 1,000 employees. Many sectors had more than 1 petabyte in mean stored data per company. To put the term "one petabyte" into context, at the time the report was issued, one petabyte could have stored four digital copies of the entire archives of the Library of Congress, with room to spare.[2] Most companies have plenty of raw data lying around. In fact, these days we're more likely to be drowning in data then lacking it. However, having data on hand and separating the signal from the noise so we can make informed decisions are two very different things.

ASK THE RIGHT QUESTIONS

The start of making data-informed decisions is to make sure you are asking the right questions. As an example, consider the classic marketing story from the 1970s battle of the cola titans: Coca-Cola vs Pepsi.

Coca-Cola has long had an iconic bottle design that is instantly recognizable and is an asset to Coca-Cola's enviably strong brand. Pepsi, thinking that people bought more Coke than Pepsi because they liked Coke's bottle more, decided it needed to do something about this. In 1970, John Sculley was hired as a marketing executive at PepsiCo. His first assignment: to develop a distinctive glass bottle to compete against Coke's popular 6.5-ounce container.

Had John Sculley not been the creative, curious individual he is, he surely would have headed down the same path of failure as those before him: trying to come up with a 6.5-ounce glass bottle that had as strong a brand identity as Coca-Cola's. His process might have gone something like this:

1. Design a new 6.5-ounce bottle.
2. Test out among consumers.
3. Find data revealing they still prefer the Coke bottle design.
4. Go back to Step 1, repeat until you get fired or moved to another project.

And John did design a new Pepsi bottle, which he then sent out to consumers for testing. When Pepsi went to drop off more soda and collect feedback from consumers who had agreed to be testers in exchange for free Pepsi, John realized something interesting. All the Pepsi was being consumed.

This was the moment he recognized the actual problem he was trying to solve. Instead of designing a better 6.5-ounce glass bottle, Sculley realized it made more sense to design a much bigger bottle, and avoid going head-to-head with the smaller Coke product. In this way, Pepsi would boost its profits, since the company earned more when consumers drank more of its soda, and with a larger bottle design shoppers could obtain more of what they wanted.[3]

He invented the two-liter soda bottle. Besides allowing consumers to purchase soda in larger quantities, the bottle was also preferred by emerging superstores like Wal-Mart because it was made of plastic rather than glass. Up until that point, Wal-Mart had not even stocked soda because of the hassle of stocking fragile glass bottles. The story, which appeared as an article in *Business Management Daily,* goes that the then-30-year-old Sculley met with retail legend Sam Walton to convince him to stock Pepsi's new bottle in his Wal-Mart stores.

> "Mr. Walton, here is our new unbreakable bottle for Pepsi, and we think it's perfect for your superstores," Sculley said.
> Then he intentionally dropped the bottle.

Walton expected it to create a mess. But when the bottle bounced slightly off the floor and rolled harmlessly a few feet, Walton was stunned.

"What is that bottle made of?" Walton asked in amazement.

"That was the beginning of our most successful marketing campaign," Sculley says.[4]

One tension we will continually discuss throughout this chapter is being data *informed* vs data *driven*. The key is to answer the right questions with the right type of information.

Sculley used data to aid his decision-making, but he did not let data make the decisions for him. He used his own judgment to complement what the data was showing him. Had he been data driven, he would have kept heading down dead ends that would have only yielded incremental increases in the amount of Pepsi sold. Rather, Sculley was able to innovate and turn Pepsi into a goliath, which ultimately helped him land the CEO job at Apple Computer. (To be fair, as you may recall, he had a less successful tenure at Apple.)

THE IMPORTANCE OF DATA SCIENCE

With the buzzwords "Big Data" so ubiquitous, you probably feel increasing pressure to do something with the data you have. And it's true that leveraging data is increasingly important to informing strategic decisions for optimal performance. The professional world's new obsession with big data can be seen starkly in the skyrocketing popularity of "data science" as a new job description.

Over the last few decades data science has become a hotly pursued role in most companies.[5] In 2012, the cover of the *Harvard Business Review,* reflecting on the increasing demand for these professionals, exclaimed, "Data Scientist: The Sexiest Job of the 21st Century."[6]

While the public perception of data scientists may be that they are number-crunching robots, their jobs go well beyond staring at spreadsheets all day. In fact, being any kind of scientist requires a lot of creative thinking. The creativity emerges in their ability to ask the right questions when they

analyze data. A great data scientist will be able to help your company optimize around its long-term vision and goals, rather than just recommending
small improvements in product-specific features.

LINKEDIN

Two of the earliest organizations to have a formal "data science" function
were among our chosen companies for analysis: Facebook, led by Jeff Ham-
merbacher, and LinkedIn, led by DJ Patil. In fact, Jeff and DJ actually
coined the term "data scientist" in one of their first meetings.[7]

In about three years, LinkedIn had grown the number of accounts on
its platform to eight million professionals, a remarkable feat. But their real
challenge was engaging those accounts. One LinkedIn manager at the time
described the LinkedIn experience as "arriving at a conference reception and
realizing you don't know anyone. So you just stand in the corner sipping
your drink—and you probably leave early."[8]

Jonathan Goldman, who joined LinkedIn after getting a PhD in phys-
ics from Stanford, started looking at all of the data LinkedIn had about its
members through the lens of engagement. He quickly realized that one easy
way to prevent users from feeling like they didn't know anyone was for the
service to make smarter recommendations of other people they might know.

The solution was in the data. The feature, which would later be called
PYMK (for People You May Know), was novel at the time. As DJ Patil
explained:

> It's easy for software to predict that if James knows Mary, and Mary knows
> John Smith, then James may know John Smith. (Well, conceptually easy.
> Finding connections in graphs gets tough quickly as the endpoints get
> farther apart. But solving that problem is what data scientists are for.) But
> imagine searching for John Smith by name on a network with hundreds
> of millions of users![9]

While today PYMK is a common feature on social networks, Goldman
was its pioneer. At the time, he actually struggled to get the engineering

group to build it out, as they were focused on other challenges around scaling. But he did convince LinkedIn founder Reid Hoffman (who was also, at the time, CEO) to let him run some experiments in which Goldman used the advertising slots on the site to make PYMK recommendations. The reaction was extremely positive; in fact, the "people you may know" prompts across the site actually received a 30 percent higher response rate than any other previous attempt to increase engagement. Based on those results, Goldman convinced management to roll PYMK out as a standard feature for everyone.[10]

This is a great example of using data across a project from start to finish. First, it was used to define the engagement challenge: specifically, that LinkedIn members didn't have enough connections. In doing this, Goldman took the critical and difficult step of finding what actually needed to be further measured and examined. He realized that while user growth was important, it would mean nothing without more user engagement—a pivotal insight for the nascent network.

Next, Goldman practiced good data analysis by coming up with a hypothesis on how the company could increase user engagement. To do this, he looked at the LinkedIn connections to come up with a data-based approach to recommend "people you may know."

After forming his hypothesis, he proceeded to run an experiment using the advertising slots to create data, with the results of the experiment demonstrating how effective his approach was at solving the problem he set out to solve (helping people find more connections), which, finally, would either validate or invalidate his hypothesis.

The results of these experiments allowed him to go to company leadership with evidence that he had uncovered what might possibly be a really amazing way to increase user engagement. By providing this evidence to company leadership, he made it easy for them to ask the development team to focus on the addition of a new feature for LinkedIn.

While not every product solution will involve using data to create products, the steps of using data in formulating hypotheses and then validating/invalidating them through experimentation are very common tools for key decisions.

FACEBOOK

Facebook uses a similar approach. As Adam Mosseri, a product designer at Facebook, notes: "Data helps us understand how users use our products, and how we can optimize them."

He starts, though, by pointing out that "at Facebook we use data to inform certain types of decisions but are also very skeptical of being overly data driven." Adam's talk in September of 2010 was actually the first time I heard this contrast between being *data informed* and *data driven*—but it immediately resonated with me, as you can see.

Adam uses the example of re-engineering the process for uploading photos at Facebook. The company had just changed the process two months before the talk I attended. Specifically, Facebook had a solution that required the installation of a plug-in to upload images. While the company had done a lot to create a compelling experience once that plug-in was installed, of the 1.1 million people a day who were urged to install the plug-in, only 37 percent ever tried.

I should emphasize here up front that photos are one of the most important types of content for Facebook. While textual updates matter, you only need to look at the "average" Facebook user to understand how critical photos are to the system. A significant portion of a user's attention is given to scanning images of their friends' Friday nights. If that doesn't convince you, keep in mind that Facebook paid $1 billion less than two years after Adam's talk to acquire Instagram—because it had a mobile-first approach to uploading photos in real time.

In fact, at the time of Adam's talk, Facebook had just recently passed the 50-billion mark on photos uploaded; it was the largest photo site on the Internet. Three years later that trend had continued, with Facebook storing more than 250 billion photos and adding an average of 350 million a day.[11]

So anyway, Facebook switched to using the operating system's default file upload functionality to allow users to select photos to upload. As the company optimized this process, it significantly exceeded the results from the prior approach over time. Specifically, it went from 34 percent of successful uploads per attempt to 48 percent over two months.

This broke down as follows:

- 87% reach the page which allowed them to upload (things like page load time or not having Flash installed resulted in the first 13% decay)
- 57% actually selected photos
- 52% clicked the upload button
- 48% were successful (bugs, page load)

It's actually the next step in their process that I want to highlight, though. As Facebook went along optimizing the interaction and workflow (resulting in a 14 percent increase in successful uploads), it quickly optimized and reduced the number of steps required, and gradually increased photos uploaded.

However, the company encountered a "local maximum" that it was not able to break through until it actually did something very counterintuitive: The company added a step to the process. Specifically, as it analyzed the data, Facebook realized that 85 percent of users were only uploading one photo per album. In almost every case, this was very likely the result of users being unsure how or even if they could select more than one file per upload.

So Facebook added a screen, only shown once, which explained that in order to select multiple photographs to be uploaded, you could hold down the CTRL or Shift key while clicking on files.

Once the company added the tutorial to explain how to select multiple files, the number of people who uploaded only one file decreased to 40 percent. Facebook only showed each user the tutorial until he/she successfully uploaded more than one file. According to Adam's presentation, this one step increased the total average photos per upload attempt from 3 to 11.

When you realize the data above encompasses millions of upload attempts, this almost fourfold increase materially changed the number of photos in the Facebook system and created a much better experience for Facebook customers.[12]

It's not just the photos team. Facebook product designer Cemre Güngör, the founder of the startup Branch, one year after his company was acquired by Facebook and he joined the team, wrote a post on the service Medium that talked about his experience. He stated that the goal of his post was to explain "what I would have loved to know before starting my new job."

Interestingly, one of the things he would have loved to have known up front was that "data isn't a silver bullet":

> A lot of product decisions for brand new startup projects are done with gut feeling, because usually that's all the available information there is. After operating this way for many years, I was looking forward to being able to harness all the data about how people use News Feed.
>
> I quickly found out that the potential of data doesn't necessarily render it easier to make decisions. Sometimes it turns out you aren't measuring the right thing, and new data will take time to gather. Sometimes the data that comes out is contradictory or inaccurate. And even when the data seems correct, it only explains what is happening, not the why. This critical question is still up to interpretation, so there can still be some amount of gut feeling involved.[13]

AIRBNB GROWTH WITH PHOTOGRAPHY

Coming back to the subject of photos, they are involved in another great story from our case studies. In this case, though, it's professional photos and the impact they had on improving the Airbnb experience, as explained in a talk by Joe Zadeh, the director of product at Airbnb.

Zadeh starts by explaining that when Airbnb was in Y Combinator, Paul Graham told the young company's founders they needed to go to where their customers were. At the time, a lot of their customers were in NYC. So they got on a plane and went to NYC.

As they started meeting different customers, they developed a hypothesis: "Hosts who post pictures taken by professional photographers will get more business." In December of 2010, they quickly set to test this theory by getting about 100 professional shots in just a few different cities and allowed hosts to use these photos on their listings.

After looking at the data, they realized that their theory was in fact correct. Professionally photographed listings got two to three times as many bookings as the average host's location.

They responded with what is often called a "concierge MVP"—in other words, a version of the product in which a person (the concierge) does the work, which is later automated using software support. In this case, they had an employee communicate with hosts and professional photographers via email, and used a simple spreadsheet to track progress and a Dropbox folder to share the professionally photographed pictures.

Over time Airbnb has replaced the employee with software automating the processes. As the system scaled, host locations that were professionally photographed continued to see better sales performance.

Airbnb now has 30 photographers just in the city of London and has continued to see tremendous growth driven by these professional photographs.

Joe credits Paul Graham and the team at Y Combinator, saying, "It all starts by meeting your users."[14]

DON'T FORGET ABOUT QUALITATIVE DATA

This leads to the next important point, which is that you shouldn't overlook *qualitative* data just because so much *quantitative* data is available in our digital world. At a minimum, this qualitative data can add the story to the information you are analyzing and ensure you make the leap to new areas to optimize when you get the chance.

When LinkedIn first launched, the company would actually follow up with individual members who got invitations and didn't accept them.[15] It also had a natural flow of qualitative feedback, given co-founder Reid Hoffman's network. As Konstantin Guericke, another of LinkedIn's co-founders, explained:

> [T]he great thing about this particular business is that Reid [Hoffman, LinkedIn's CEO] and I would always have lunch with one of our contacts, people that we know, that's how we network. So during lunch people would naturally give us feedback. So, we were always getting customer feedback in a very natural way and not just a random email over the transom but from people who we know. We could ask follow-up questions, so that was very helpful.[16]

Using this kind of qualitative data also ensures you don't get caught slicing the data to find results that don't really exist. There probably is no concept more easily recited, yet less understood, from most individuals' high-school statistics class than the phrase "correlation does not imply causation." It's just so tempting to see correlations in the data and assume there must be some relationship.

Many of the companies in our study used A/B testing or controlled experiments in which they showed slightly different versions of the product to two different segments of customers. Jan Overgoor, a data scientist at Airbnb, explained:

> The outside world often has a much larger effect on metrics than product changes do. Users can behave very differently depending on the day of week, the time of year, the weather (especially in the case of a travel company like Airbnb), or whether they learned about the website through an online ad or found the site organically. Controlled experiments isolate the impact of the product change while controlling for the aforementioned external factors.[17]

Especially when it comes to product changes, you need both qualitative and quantitative data to tell the whole story. Let's go back to the Facebook News Feed example (from Chapter 9). Back in 2007, when Facebook created what is now the standard home page for all users—News Feed—the qualitative reports showed that users hated it! While News Feed actually didn't expose any information that an active Facebook user couldn't already discover, it did make this information much easier to see, and left many Facebook users feeling exposed. For example, before News Feed, if you changed your relationship status, someone would have to go look at your page to find out. With News Feed, that information was being broadcast to all your connections. This caused serious consternation among many Facebook users. In fact, they hated it so much that Facebook groups with names such as "I Hate the News Feed" were created, and these groups attracted hundreds of thousands of users. The feature garnered some bad press for Facebook, with publications such as *Time* magazine claiming "Generation Facebook takes action against Facebook."

If judged only by qualitative feedback, News Feed would have been instantly recalled as a disastrous feature. However, the quantitative data showed a different story. Overall, user engagement was increased. While wall posts did take a hit, comments skyrocketed.[18]

Which is why you need to strive to gather both types of data. The picture is incomplete if you lack either qualitative data or quantitative data, leading you to make decisions based on a partial, rather than a complete understanding, of what is occurring.

AUTOMATTIC

Of the companies we analyzed, Automattic provides a great example of how a similar mix of qualitative and quantitative data can inform the product development process. On its corporate website, the company describes this process as "data-informed, user-driven" and goes on to elaborate:

> For every feature we launch, we gather metrics about its usage, interaction, and growth in addition to listening to the masses of feedback we get on our blog and through support. This helps us inform decisions about where things need to go. It's not uncommon to launch a feature and then revise it several times over the next week.[19]

In Scott Berkun's book about his year working at Automattic, *The Year without Pants,* he confirms that this is more than just corporate speak. He explains that *before* beginning work on a given feature, the team will spend time contemplating what data they will collect after it's launched.

> Consider what data will tell you it works. Since it's a live service, learn from what users are doing. The plan for a new feature must consider how its positive or negative impact on customers can be measured. For example, if the goal is to improve the number of comments bloggers get from readers, we'd track how many comments visitors write each day before and after the change.[20]

After doing the development and deploying the solution, the programming team comes back to "learn" again in a data-informed way:

> Data is captured instantly and discussed, often hourly, by the folks who did the work. Bugs are found and fixed. For larger features, several rounds of revisions are made to the design.[21]

GOOGLE

Whenever I bring up the principle of being data informed but not data driven, I get pushback from people who look at Google and say, isn't that a completely data-driven company? My short answer is, not from what we've read and observed. In the book *How Google Works,* co-author Eric Schmidt, longtime CEO and now executive chairman of Google, talks about his ideal employee, and one quality he emphasizes is how that employee deals with data: "She is analytically smart. She is comfortable with data and can use it to make decisions. She also understands its fallacies and is wary of endless analysis. Let data decide, she believes, but don't let it take over."[22]

AIRBNB

Airbnb is another company that fosters a culture of experimentation, through which it seeks to uncover both qualitative and quantitative evidence of the success or failure of its initiatives.

While it can be difficult to argue for experimentation when it appears things are working or are good to go for production, the importance of continuing to experiment is not to be underestimated. Airbnb found this out when working on a redesign of the website's search feature.

After putting in a ton of work to design the new search page and doing numerous qualitative user studies, all of which yielded positive results, the company then set out to do a quantitative experiment.

> A lot of work went into the project, and we all thought it was clearly better; our users agreed in qualitative user studies. Despite this, we wanted to evaluate the new design quantitatively with an experiment. This can be

hard to argue for, especially when testing a big new product like this. It can feel like a missed marketing opportunity if we don't launch to everyone at the same time. However, to keep in the spirit of our testing culture, we did test the new design—to measure the actual impact and, more importantly, gather knowledge about which aspects did and didn't work.[23]

Despite all the positive qualitative feedback, the initial experiments yielded a neutral result—that is, there was no discernible difference between the old design and the new design. The team, feeling this could not be right, decided to break down the results to see where their hypothesis had gone wrong.

It turned out that the new design had caused a glitch for Internet Explorer users, and that their now incredibly negative experience with the search feature was dragging down the results of what was otherwise a very successful redesign. Had the experiment testing the design not been done, the glitch might not have been caught early on, and the negative impact could have been much larger.[24]

While the problem posed in this example was easy to figure out, the larger point is you need to be careful that your experiment actually validates what you are exploring. With a travel platform, outside factors such as time of year or weather can have a significant impact on metrics like conversion rates as well.

However, this rule does not apply only to Internet companies. The challenge of results that can't be replicated spans many disciplines. In September of 2011, *Nature Reviews Drug Discovery* published an analysis[25] by Dr. Khusru Asadullah and his colleagues at Bayer that tested

> . . . 67 target-validation projects, covering the majority of Bayer's work in oncology, women's health and cardiovascular medicine over the past 4 years. Of these, results from internal experiments matched up with the published findings in only 14 projects, but were highly inconsistent in 43 (in a further 10 projects, claims were rated as mostly reproducible, partially reproducible or not applicable).

This means that only about 25 percent of the published research Bayer tried to replicate (and theoretically build upon) could actually be replicated in the lab. In the other three out of four experiments, the results were "highly inconsistent." While surprising to me, this apparently isn't a new phenomenon, as the article in *Nature* goes on to cite other published studies that show similar challenges in replicating results.

The *Wall Street Journal* covered the same phenomenon, summarizing it as "one of medicine's dirty secrets," and adding, "Most results, including those that appear in top-flight peer-reviewed journals, can't be reproduced."[26]

John Ioannidis from Stanford University's School of Medicine has spent considerable time investigating what is causing this. In 2005, he wrote a paper titled "Why Most Published Research Findings Are False"[27] in which he walks through six factors that contribute to these false positives. While the first four come down to how the experiment was designed and the number of observations being used to infer the findings, the last two are the most interesting to me, because they touch on the psychology of the researcher. Specifically, Ioannidis finds a decrease in the likelihood the research is true if the researcher has skewed financial and other interests, and if the field is "hotter" or has more scientific teams involved.

AVOID "DATA PUKING"

One final caution: Many organizations fall into the trap of confusing simply *having* data with actually *analyzing* it. This is so prevalent that the term "data puking" was coined to describe simply publishing a lot of data without a lot of analysis.

The first to use the term "data puking" was Google's digital marketing evangelist, Avinash Kaushik, in a blog post[28] in which he explained the difference between web analysis and web reporting.

In the post, Avinash explains that simple activities—like setting up Google Analytics to capture data, how many visits your webpage got, what traffic channel they came through (direct, organic, email), or time spent on page—are not really going to help you much without data analysis, which helps you to understand the context of the data and identify actions to take based on that context.

The difference between analysis and reporting is, fortunately, easy to check. If you are doing good data analysis, your data should be providing you with insights into your company's key performance indicators (KPIs), actions you can take based on these insights, and what the potential impact of these actions might be.[29] If there are no such recommendations, you're looking at data reporting—or, worse, data puking.

If you are the one coming up with these recommendations, it's important that you dress your data up appropriately for the audience reviewing it. Don't just show an intimidating spreadsheet with rows upon rows of data; rather, try and break it down into a much more digestible format, such as a PowerPoint slide that uses well-thought-out headers and bullet point lists. Doing so will greatly increase your chance of being heard!

PUTTING THIS INTO ACTION

Question 1: What are the critical metrics for your business?

As discussed throughout this chapter, organizations are drowning in data. The first step to creating a really data-informed organization is to make sure you have alignment on the critical metrics for your organization.

I've found a helpful question to ask when searching for clarity on these metrics is: Assuming success, what numbers will you use to explain that success in three years? As you start to unpack that vision of the future it's those numbers that are often the critical metrics for your business—and sometimes they are not about revenue.

For example, I imagine that both YouTube and Revver would have talked about the number of videos being stored and viewed on their services as key metrics for their future, rather than advertising dollars generated through their platforms. On the other hand, Tesla and Fisker certainly would have talked about the number of cars sold.

Question 2: What are the right goals for these metrics?

Once you've identified the key metrics, it's important to make sure your whole team understands up front what success looks like. You need to be aggressive, but being irrationally so leads to danger.

No company from our chosen sets illustrates the danger of irrational projections more than Fisker. In January 2008, at the North American International Auto Show in Detroit, Fisker announced its first vehicle. The company's press release announcing the car said:

> Initial deliveries of the Karma will commence in the 4th quarter of 2009, with annual production projected to reach 15,000 cars. The first 99 cars off the assembly line will be individually numbered and signed by Henrik Fisker and will be produced in the color and trim of the show car seen at NAIAS.[30]

This would prove to be incredibly optimistic—both in terms of the timeframe (production didn't commence until the middle of 2011) and the estimated number of cars sold. Based on analysis of documents from Fisker's bankruptcy filing in 2013, it appears the company sold a total of roughly 2,000 cars across its life, before declaring bankruptcy.[31] In retrospect, the 15,000-car projection looks even more ludicrous when you consider that the Karma had a base price of $80,000, placing it in the luxury sedan market. To call the projection an aggressive goal is being generous. For perspective, let's look at other luxury vehicle sales numbers. Consider the Audi A8, a luxury sedan with a similar reputation for great design at a relatively similar price—in 2013 and 2012, Audi sold 6,300 and 6,002 cars, respectively.[32] And Fisker's wasn't simply an abstract goal—the company used it as a milestone for tranches of investments, and even paid some of its suppliers for 15,000 parts up front.[33] Ultimately, the use of these projections for procurement and financing decisions contributed to Fisker's cash flow challenges and bankruptcy.

Question 3: How can you best publicly display the metrics used?

Once aligned around these key metrics, the next step is to make the results publicly available to the entire organization on a regular basis. This can be done in different ways depending on the organization's culture, but popular techniques include regular emails in which the data is shared or regularly scheduled meetings to announce metrics measurements.

One of the best ways to do this is by using a digital dashboard displaying results updated in real time. As Joe Zadeh of Airbnb said, in his talk on the impact of professional photos (mentioned earlier):

> If I could leave you with one piece of advice, it is build a dashboard. If you need the metrics today, you are going to need the metrics tomorrow, three weeks from now, one year from now, three years from now . . . actually, make it pretty.[34]

A great way to incorporate the use of dashboards is to have the key metrics for that week, month, or quarter displayed with a dashboard in a public space, such as on TVs around the office. This transparency helps employees to see if they are making progress and understand how their progress is being measured. In addition, having a public display of metrics is a refreshing example of transparency for any organization. The public display allows everyone to get on board with what the metrics of an organization are and leaves no doubt as to what an employee's efforts should be focused on achieving.

Question 4: How can you encourage a culture of experimentation?

John Sculley, the inventor of the two-liter Pepsi bottle and former CEO of Apple, when asked for his favorite piece of advice, responded, "Be curious . . . If you're insatiably curious, you are always observing, questioning, and wondering, and that's what sets extraordinary entrepreneurs apart."[35]

Curiosity generally leads to experimentation. And experimentation is crucial to growth. Any organization that is seeking to grow and continually innovate needs to foster a culture of experimentation to see if what it is doing is actually working.

11

FINANCING STRATEGIES

"Cash flow is like the blood flow in our bodies. Interruption or restriction will cause a perfectly healthy body to rapidly deteriorate."

—Unknown

TECHNOLOGY ENTREPRENEURS AND INVESTORS ARE QUICK TO POINT OUT how much less expensive it is to start a company today compared to a decade ago. I've experienced this firsthand, both as an entrepreneur and investor. The first company I founded had seven-figure up-front expenses—including acquiring Dell servers that had to be racked in two different datacenters for redundancy well before our first customer ever used the solution. During the time we ran that business, Amazon dramatically improved its cloud computing offerings; by the time we sold the business to LinkedIn, all those servers had been sold for pennies on the dollar and we were doing semantic processing on over a million content items per day (blog posts and news articles) for a few hundred dollars a month, on credit card expense from Amazon.

Beyond the changing infrastructure (from a fixed capital expense to an ongoing "pay as you go" service expense), software developers can now also incorporate a lot of third-party libraries, dramatically simplifying what used to be very complex processes. For example, instead of having to write all the code needed in order to send an SMS message from a program, you can incorporate a few lines of Twilio code and leverage all the work they have done. Not only does this save weeks of engineering up front, but as with Amazon's cloud computing offering, the solution can easily scale as the product usage increases. For example, Uber still uses Twilio to deliver text messages to customers around the world about the status of their ride.[1]

Finally, in terms of getting distribution for mobile applications, you can create an app and quickly get mobile distribution to most mobile phones without any conversations with phone carriers, thanks to Apple and Google's app stores. Entrepreneurs often complain to me about the multi-week process required to get their application approved by Apple's App Store review, but I'm quick to remind them that's nothing relative to sitting in windowless conference rooms for meeting after meeting with carriers over months, if not years, to get your application onto the carrier's deck. That was the process, before Apple democratized the home screen with its App Store.

All of these trends have made it truly much less expensive to start a software company today. It's not just software companies, though. People creating physical products are realizing some of the same cost benefits early in their development by leveraging 3D printers and other rapid-prototyping techniques. They are also getting better access to innovators and early adopters thanks to communities like Kickstarter and Indiegogo. The scale of these communities is impressive. While not everything on Kickstarter's platform is a business venture, the company reports that 9 million people have participated in over 88,000 projects since the company was founded, donating over $1.8 billion.[2]

Early experiments around a specific startup idea are much less expensive than they were a generation ago. While this is a tremendous advantage, it is still very expensive to successfully scale a startup.

None of our chosen companies illustrate this point better than Tumblr. The first investment was $750,000, and lasted about 18 months. Early investor and board member Bijan Sabet commented on his blog:

> During the first 12–15 months following the investment we saw user growth for sure. But it wasn't a significant steep curve by any measure. I believe we had something like 450K registered users by the end of 2008.

That's impressive considering it was just David and Marco but it wasn't earth shattering.

In the same post, Sabet looked at some of the lessons learned after the company started scaling rapidly. One was the importance of patience, while the team worked through these early iterations. This early patience was matched by an aggressive financing strategy through which Tumblr ultimately raised over $125 million across the next four financing rounds.

As we discussed in the prerequisites section, patience is important up front to avoid scaling prematurely. However, after a company has experienced one or more catalyzing growth events, and is scaling rapidly, it rarely achieves its desired growth through organic cash flow alone.

As a VC, this is good news for me, as it means many startups will still need capital to grow. Still, not every dollar is created equal, and therefore you need to be very analytical about how you invest in growth. While there is no one-size-fits-all playbook for this, developing the right financing strategy for your company is crucial to realizing your company's full potential.

Each of the companies we researched had to figure out the correct financing strategy. Let's look at some of the more interesting examples, below.

MCDONALD'S: A REAL-ESTATE TYCOON

In his thoroughly researched book *McDonald's: Behind the Arches,* John Love explains:

> Because of [VP of Finance Harry] Sonneborn's creative financing, McDonald's grew much faster than chains that thought it prudent to avoid "excessive" debt. White Castle had started in the hamburger business thirty years before [Ray] Kroc and, like McDonald's, it built a reputation for strong restaurant operations. But its growth was stymied by conservative financing. Indeed, the only thing that explains White Castle's failure to capitalize on its head start in the hamburger business was founder E.W. "Billy" Ingram's strict policy against borrowing.[3]

While the willingness to take a more aggressive stance on financing certainly was key, at least as impressive, in my research on McDonald's financing history, is how creative the company was in coming up with structures to finance that leverage.

The model used for financing actually started with one of Kroc's core beliefs on which he refused to compromise: He would not make money by charging a markup to the McDonald's franchisees for the supplies they would need to operate their stores. This was quite unusual for a restaurant franchise group at the time. Kroc explained that he wanted to "help the individual operator succeed in every way" he could, saying that the franchisees' "success would insure my success. But I couldn't do that and, at the same time, treat him as a customer. There is a basic conflict in trying to treat a man as a partner on the one hand while selling him something at a profit on the other."

This constraint led to the creative idea that ultimately allowed McDonald's to grow so quickly. Rather than profit from the supplies being sold to their stores, McDonald's would go into the real-estate business.

Specifically, they would first lease and then later purchase the land on which the stores were constructed, and lease the property back to the franchise operators. These operators would pay either a percentage of the store's sales or a base rent, calculated as a markup on the cost of financing the land—whichever was higher. This allowed the company to share in the profits of the store, while still having a guaranteed minimum cash flow to cover the cost of the financing.

Interestingly, the idea originated with Harry Sonneborn, while he still worked at Tastee-Freez (mentioned in Chapter 2). When he proposed the idea to his then employers, they weren't interested, since Tastee-Freez was making a tidy profit selling ice cream mix supplies to its franchisees. Later, Sonneborn would often frame McDonald's as a real-estate business more than a restaurant.

This characterization upset Kroc, who was very passionate about the restaurant business, and how these franchises were run. Interestingly, it was that passion for operations that originally made the structure appealing to Kroc. In McDonald's early days, franchise agreements were a relatively new concept, without a lot of case law around them, but leases on land were a standard agreement, and allowed Kroc to control the experience much more than the franchise agreements ever would. After all, he owned the property.

The real-estate model allowed McDonald's to grow quickly, eclipsing competitors like White Castle, but even this model did not provide enough cash to support the company's tremendous growth. The finance team at McDonald's continued to search for additional sources to accelerate that growth. Ultimately, in 1960, the company convinced two insurance companies to loan the business $1.5 million at 7 percent interest, in exchange for 20 percent of the company to split, plus an additional 2.5 percent stock fee for the broker of the deal. After McDonald's went public in 1965, the insurance companies sold that stock for almost $20 million, making it a fantastic investment, but had the companies held their position until today it would be worth over $2 billion. While the loan was expensive capital for McDonald's, it allowed the company to continue its explosive growth and ultimately enabled it to go public and continue growing in the public markets, while most of its competitors had to sell to larger companies or, like White Castle, remain relatively modest businesses.

BE CAREFUL OF OPPORTUNISTIC FINANCING

Sometimes the opposite is true. Instead of a financing window slamming shut, there are programs or opportunities that make it quite easy to raise an abundant amount of capital. This was the situation both Tesla and Fisker found themselves in when the Department of Energy created the Advanced Technology Vehicle Manufacturing (ATVM) program in the fall of 2008. The government created the program to provide $25 billion in low-interest loans to manufacturers producing energy-efficient cars. The catch was that the loans had to be directed to the creation or improvement of the company's manufacturing facilities.

Ray Lane, a prominent investor in Fisker through his fund Kleiner Perkins, commented in an interview that this was part of his thesis when he ultimately invested in Fisker:

> When I did Fisker and another car company, my partners thought I was
> out of my mind. But I had a thesis. We can invest in a car company

and either have a way to get the valuation high enough so you don't get crushed on dilution, or get low-cost loans that are high leverage for equity investors.[4]

Both Fisker and Tesla qualified for the program in 2009, and began to draw money against the loans. However, this is where their paths diverged. Tesla was a couple years more mature as a company and was able to use the loans as intended—and ultimately pay the loan back nine years early, with interest. On the other hand, Fisker, while it received a similar loan commitment from the government, was unable to meet the milestones necessary to allow it to continue to draw down that commitment.

Unfortunately, Fisker was not ready to take advantage of the program's low-cost loans because the firm was still over two years away from being ready to manufacture the car. As mentioned in the last chapter, the company's projections were very unrealistic, and it was never able to use the leverage the government program should have provided.

The point as it relates to financing is that, as an entrepreneur, your overall business strategy should not be driven exclusively by the financing options available. I can't imagine how tempting it was for the Fisker Board of Directors to grab this low-interest loan. Especially if some of them (as Ray Lane implied in the interview mentioned earlier) had used programs like this as part of their investment thesis. However, sometimes you have to walk away from those "easier" options and come up with alternatives.

As discussed in the prerequisites section of this book, sometimes this requires insane perseverance from the founders. While Tesla was able to take advantage of the low-interest loans when the program was available, given the company's progress, if Elon Musk had not personally written the $3 million check before Christmas 2008 the company would have never survived.

Even more difficult, turning down money that comes with strings attached that are bad for the business means that sometimes you have to go through periods of organic growth. The closest thing to a company that financed its growth organically, among our chosen case studies, was Cvent.

While Cvent quickly raised $17 million from a variety of DC-area angel investors and venture funds (including the firm I now work at, Birchmere Ventures), the macroeconomic environment changed rapidly between the dot-com bubble bursting and September 11, severely impacting corporate event travel as an industry.

As discussed in Chapter 2, founder Reggie Aggarwal and his team had to make dramatic changes to cut expenses and grow organically until the company's financing prospects increased. The company maintained that organic growth for a decade, until it announced its $136 million growth financing shortly before it went public at a valuation of over a billion dollars.[5]

PUTTING THIS INTO ACTION

Question 1: What are the milestones that truly drive value creation and how much cash is necessary to hit those milestones?

As you demonstrate growth and success, your business's value doesn't usually increase steadily quarter after quarter at a linear rate. There are specific events in each business that cause *step-function changes* in the value of the business. To give an easy example, at the earliest stages of a startup's development, when no one is using its product, the company's valuation will be low, but after its first customers start to use and see value from its product, the company's valuation will be dramatically higher.

The key to a successful fundraising strategy is to understand where those step functions are and raise enough money to get past those milestones, while also including enough runway to successfully complete additional financing after that event.

Question 2: Are you mentally prepared for the asymmetry of fundraising?

One thing that surprises most entrepreneurs is how many rejections most startups face, even in a "successful" financing. It's easy to read about a company stepping out and raising a large round of investment and assume the event was painless.

In fact, most financing involves hearing "no" a lot before getting that critical "yes." In an ideal world, you will have a few different firms interested in financing your startup, so you can negotiate and play them against each other to ultimately land on the right partner with what you feel are good terms.

Even the fastest-growing companies sometimes face challenges getting new investors aligned on fair terms. When I first started making this argument, my students were quick to point out that it's probably true for everyone except Facebook.

Certainly, Facebook had a lot of leverage during most of its financing rounds. For example, Jim Breyer, a partner at Accel Partners, shared recently that when he and Mark Zuckerberg were negotiating terms for Facebook's $12.7 million Series A investment in May of 2005, he thought he could probably get the deal done at a $70 million pre-money valuation, but ultimately, for the sake of speed, came in at $78 million. With what we know today, that looks like an amazing deal, and even at the time Facebook's fantastic growth rate made it a straightforward negotiation in which Facebook consistently had the upper hand.[6]

However, it only recently became public how challenging it was for Facebook to raise its $200 million growth round in May of 2009. Marc Andreesen, a longtime board member of the firm, recently shared that after the financial crisis, Facebook found it difficult to get a price close to Microsoft's October 2007 valuation of $15 billion. In fact, the company was very close to raising money at a $3 billion valuation. They were spared having to take the reduced valuation by Russian entrepreneur and venture capitalist Yuri Millner, who invested in the company at a $10 billion valuation. However, as emphasized above, after a bunch of investors passed or presented offers with which Facebook was not happy, the company finally found the terms it was looking for, and lived to grow.[7]

Another interesting example comes from Airbnb co-founder and CEO Brian Chesky, who recently published a post on the service Medium that described his financing experience:

> On June 26, 2008, our friend Michael Seibel introduced us to 7 prominent investors in Silicon Valley. We were attempting to raise $150,000 at a $1.5M valuation. That means for $150,000 you could have bought 10% of Airbnb . . . The other 2 did not reply.

The investors that rejected us were smart people, and I am sure we didn't look very impressive at the time.

Next time you have an idea and it gets rejected, I want you to think of [this].[8]

Obviously, today 10 percent of Airbnb would be an incredibly valuable investment and I'm sure all of those investors regret passing on the opportunity. I'd like to focus on it from Brian's perspective though—he did figure out a way to continue financing the business shortly after these rejections, joining Y Combinator in January of 2009 and ultimately going on to raise over $2 billion in venture capital.[9]

This misunderstanding of how easy it is to raise venture capital is so prevalent, I'd like to share one final example. The week after LinkedIn went public, Lee Hower (director of corporate development from the company's inception through its early growth phases) wrote an article for *Fortune* magazine, "How LinkedIn First Raised Money (and Endured Rejection)," in which he walks through LinkedIn's experience raising the Series A round. Lee explains it took "several months" and the company ended pitching to over 25 VCs to get six partner meetings and two term sheets. LinkedIn ultimately raised $4.7 million from Sequoia Capital at a "pre-money valuation between $10 million and $15 million," in effect selling roughly a third to a quarter of the company for $4.7 million of investment capital. Obviously this was a great investment for Sequoia, but the point is that LinkedIn had a 10 percent success rate from first meeting to term sheet.[10] Fundraising is a very asymmetric process.

Question 3: Have you allocated enough time to run the fundraising process?

It takes time to raise money, and it's something you'll need to do continually, at least until you no longer need outside capital to finance your growth. Ironically, it's at that point (when you don't need capital) that it will instantly become easier to finance your business. Until then, expect the overhead to be significant.

In my experience, at the earlier stages of financing (Seed, Series A & B at least) active fundraising is an almost full-time commitment for the

CEO. Beyond this, it's a significant distraction for the rest of the team. As the company matures, it typically adds other executives who can help drive the financing, but at the end of the day, financing remains one of the CEO's main responsibilities.

If you haven't allocated enough of your time, delegate some of your other priorities to make sure you can give fundraising the priority it needs.

Question 4: Once you've gotten investors' interest are you sure they are good partners for your business?

When students at Princeton asked Aaron Patzer, the founder and CEO of Mint, about his fundraising process, his answer reinforced what a long-term commitment it is to add an investor to your company. In addition to the usual diligence process, Aaron also had a long dinner with each potential investor, to get to know them as individuals and decide whether each was a "decent person." I think this is a wonderful technique and one that I've used with some of my own investments.

Another similar technique is to talk to CEOs at some of the potential investors' other portfolio companies. Entrepreneurs generally will be very transparent, as they understand the importance of this potential partnership. At Birchmere Ventures, we always offer these introductions as a way for the team at the potential investment to get a chance to know us better.

12

HIGH-PERFORMING TEAMS

"No matter how brilliant your mind or strategy, if you're playing a solo game, you'll always lose out to a team."

—Reid Hoffman[1]

I WAS BORN AND RAISED IN NORTHEAST OHIO. SPECIFICALLY, I GREW UP in a small suburb about 45 minutes south of Cleveland. It was a wonderful place to grow up. Even after moving to Pittsburgh, New York City, and back to Pittsburgh, I have remained either a loyal or insane (depending on your perspective) Cleveland sports fan.

If you don't follow professional sports, both those cities (New York and Pittsburgh) have won championships across franchises over the last few years, while the three major Cleveland teams regularly get close to a championship, only to repeatedly break our hearts with disappointing losses since 1964. This includes multiple losses in the World Series and NBA Finals, as well as the elimination of the Browns by the Denver Broncos in back-to-back years in the AFC championship games.

I bring this up, dear reader, not because it's therapeutic to complain about my teams' disappointing performances—but because Cleveland teams have lacked key elements of a high-performing team for some time.

As Cavaliers fans learned in the 2015 NBA Finals, even the best player on the planet (LeBron James), when paired with a group of terribly undermatched teammates, won't ultimately be able to deliver sustainable success—it takes a whole team. That said, it's clearly important to have superstars on the team in key positions—something the Cleveland Browns have failed to do, demonstrated repeatedly by their lack of talent at the quarterback position.

In business and in sports, you need to attract superstars, while also creating a culture in which high-performing complementary members work effectively together as a team. We talked earlier in this book about the crucial role that founders play in scaling successful startups. While it starts with the founder, as the startup grows, a group with complementary and evolving skills becomes essential.

This is certainly true when you look across the companies we explored. They are full of superstars who work together in complementary teams to achieve remarkable success. This certainly was a key ingredient to their sustained growth.

In many cases, the company's early employees have ended up staying on the team for an amazingly long time—far exceeding averages in their industries (we'll talk about this more later in this chapter). When the teams at some of these companies eventually disbanded—often because the company was acquired—the team members went on to work on other projects, experiencing amazing and continuing success.

Perhaps no company demonstrates this more than PayPal. The term "PayPal Mafia" is used with reverence in coffee shops across Silicon Valley. Since the company's sale to eBay, these early alumni of PayPal have gone on to found or invest in many of the most successful startups in the country, including LinkedIn, Tesla, and YouTube. While some of this success is certainly fueled by lessons these employees learned during their time leading PayPal, you can't overlook the raw talent of the early team.

Of course, there were certainly smart and talented team members on the comparison companies that failed. Failure is a reality in entrepreneurial endeavors, and many of these team members did remarkable things before and after working at the failed startups we studied.

As the team and I went back over our notes about our chosen companies, we discerned four common areas of emphasis that helped them deliver a high-performing team.

1. EMPHASIS ON RECRUITING PROCESS
RELEVANT FOR THEIR SITUATION

Typically, when a company starts out, it lucks into the right early hires through its existing network of connections. However, over time the ones destined for success have difficulty sustaining that serendipitous process, and the company needs to start *recruiting* talented individuals.

The question really comes down to how much of the success in hiring great people was just luck vs how much was the team's skill at hiring. There is a fascinating book by Michael Mauboussin, *The Success Equation: Untangling Skill and Luck in Business, Sports, and Investing,* which seeks to help individuals properly attribute success to skill vs luck in their different pursuits. One of the biggest insights I took from the book was the importance of having a well-defined and smart process in these pursuits.

In terms of recruiting, it was clear that a lot of our chosen companies had well-thought-out and well-defined processes. Like most of the leaders we looked at, Matt Mullenweg of Automattic/WordPress understood the importance of hiring great people. In an article he wrote for *Harvard Business Review,* he concluded:

> Nothing you do for your company has as much impact as putting the right
> people around the table. The aphorism is true: You can't manage your way
> out of a bad team. An approach to hiring that genuinely identifies real skill
> and fit will give you the best shot at assembling the right team.[2]

He preceded this statement by walking his readers through the process Automattic uses to recruit team members. It's important to point out that Automattic is a completely distributed team, so individuals literally work across the world—some even continually explore the world and check in via wi-fi cafes wherever they are.

Automattic/WordPress alum Scott Berkun explained this process in his excellent book *The Year without Pants,* which chronicled the year he spent as a team lead at Automattic and the lessons gained from that experience:

> The difference is that work at WordPress.com is done primarily, often en-tirely, online. Some people work together for months without ever being on the same continent. Teams are allowed to travel to meet a few times a year to recharge the intangibles that technology can't capture . . . But the rest of the year we worked online from wherever in the world each of us happened to be. Since location is irrelevant, Automattic, the company that runs WordPress.com, can hire the best talent in the world, wherever they are.[3]

Given this work dynamic, it's important to understand how potential candi-dates might operate in a very self-directed environment. The way Automattic tests for this is to ask candidates to spend time working on a specific project as closely related as possible to the work they'd actually do after joining the company. The candidates are paid for this work a standard rate of $25 per hour (regardless of the job they are applying for), and usually complete the work on nights and weekends so they don't have to quit their existing jobs before both sides have decided if Automattic and the candidates are a good fit. In many cases this test run can mirror the work almost perfectly, such as handling customer support issues or writing software code. In others, it's as close as possible, such as sales leaders working on presentations or doing a financial analysis of a potential deal.[4]

It's not just about having a good process, but making that process a priority, even over other company priorities. In the *Harvard Business Review* article mentioned earlier, "Tryouts Trump Interviews," Matt explains: "In our culture, overseeing a tryout takes higher priority than doing your regu-lar job; it's perfectly acceptable for people to temporarily step back from their usual work for that reason."[5]

This mindset of ensuring that a new hire is the right fit for the company as a top priority is what makes sustainable, quality, high growth possible at many of the organizations we looked at. Not only does the job applicant have to perform well during the tryout, but the people making the hiring decisions need to perform well on their talent selection, much the same way a sports team general manager is tasked with picking the right players for the type of team a coach wants to put together.

Google

Every year over one million people apply for a job at Google and the company accepts less than 0.25 percent of these applicants. For perspective, this is 25 times more selective than Harvard University's treatment of its 2012 applicants (only 6.1 percent accepted). Clearly, the challenge for Google is not getting candidates to apply, but coming up with an effective process to find the right talented individuals who will contribute.[6]

While Google takes a different approach to interviewing candidates than Automattic's "tryouts," the method is equally unique. Given its culture, Google similarly places a huge priority on key performers being involved in the interview process, and making sure they view it as a critical part of their job.

Google implemented a program that is known as the trusted-interviewer program. The idea was to turn interviewing into a privilege rather than a chore, and it immediately increased hiring and product quality across the board.

In this program, an elite team of people who were actually good at interviewing and liked to do it were given the primary duties of interviewing potential new hires. In order to determine who was good at interviewing, these prospective elite team members were scored on a variety of performance metrics, including how many interviews they had conducted, reliability (apparently some team members occasionally thought they were too elite to show up for the interview), and the quality and promptness of their feedback (Google's data showed that feedback quality is significantly worse if 48 hours have passed since the interview). The evaluation of the interviewers was then published publicly, so that others could "challenge" the incumbents and replace them if they believed their performance was better. This ability to challenge the incumbent interviewers was a key component in fostering the feeling that it was a privilege to interview. In addition to being evaluated on their ability to interview potential new hires, these product managers had to go through interview training and shadow a minimum of four interviewers as they met with candidates before being allowed to conduct interviews on their own.[7]

The process doesn't stop once a candidate accepts an offer to join the company. It also helps the candidate ramp up within the organization. At both Google and Automattic, once you are hired onto the team, unique processes are used to encourage a good onboarding experience.

In the case of Automattic, the company's creed is placed right before the signature block on an offer for a new hire, stating:

> I will never stop learning. I won't just work on things that are assigned to me. I know there's no such thing as a status quo. I will build our business sustainably through passionate and loyal customers. I will never pass up an opportunity to help out a colleague, and I'll remember the days before I knew everything. I am more motivated by impact than money, and I know that Open Source is one of the most powerful ideas of our generation. I will communicate as much as possible, because it's the oxygen of a distributed company. I am in a marathon, not a sprint, and no matter how far away the goal is, the only way to get there is by putting one foot in front of another every day. Given time, there is no problem that's insurmountable.[8]

According to Matt, founder of Automattic, this simple change has had a huge impact on the company.

In addition to reinforcing its values during the hiring process and at hiring, the company takes extra steps to ensure new hires interact directly with its customers. Once hired, employees spend their first three weeks in customer service, establishing an early connection with the people who use WordPress every single day, increasing the employees' familiarity with the company's products, and reinforcing the company's focus on building a passionate and loyal customer base. Interestingly, Automattic has also found that the responsiveness of employees during this onboarding process is a predictor of long-term success.[9]

The process for new Google employees—called "Nooglers" by the company (a combination of New and Googler)—starts with an all-day orientation. During this orientation, key executives come from different departments to talk to the Nooglers. At the orientation the Nooglers are picked up by their mentors and receive a special escort to their work areas, where they are greeted with gifts like welcome balloons and a bag of chocolates. At the end of their first week, Nooglers get to stand up and introduce themselves during the Friday all-hands meetings.[10]

2. PROVIDE LEADERSHIP CONSISTENCY

Over the last few years, venture capital firm Andreesen Horowitz has done an excellent job demonstrating the dangers of quickly replacing a founder.

In the companies we looked at, there certainly were examples in which a founder was successfully replaced with a new CEO, and other cases in which the founder scaled to ultimate success. In two of the companies mentioned above (Google and Automattic), the founder transitioned the CEO title to a "professional" only to reclaim the title years later after watching his partner operate in the role.

The more important thing is to avoid the constant turnover of executives. I found it really interesting that when a reporter asked Jonathan Abrams to briefly explain what happened to Friendster, he immediately began to talk about the instability of the leadership team. Abrams explained that Friendster had six different CEOs over the six years between first raising venture capital and ultimately being acquired. I believe there are a lot of lessons to be learned from the case study (obviously, given its prominence in this book), but it's interesting the founder's immediate reaction is not only that he was slowly transitioned out but a larger related point that the board constantly changed CEOs on a yearly average cycle for six years.[11]

In the last chapter, we talked about Reggie Aggarwal signing a personal guarantee as part of renegotiating Cvent's lease. His co-founder, Chuck Ghoorah, recalls that right before the renegotiation "Reggie got everyone around the table and said, 'Are we going to do this as a team?' And we all committed." That commitment would end up lasting longer than any of the team could have anticipated at the time. Over a decade later, after closing a $136 million growth financing round, Reggie explained to industry publication *TechCrunch,* "Eleven of our twelve senior executives have been with

Cvent since our inception." And he credited the consistency of the team with a lot of his success.[12]

Another industry publication (*Smart CEO*) explained Cvent's success:

> Aggarwal makes a point that a lot of CEOs touch on in interviews: His company's success is not all about him—it's really about his whole team. With Aggarwal, this comment feels real; in fact, the senior leaders at Cvent actually call their "secret sauce" the fact that they've stuck together as a team since the beginning.[13]

Equally amazing to me, as my team and I investigated this theme of consistency, is our discovery that about one-third of the original 100 hires are still at Google 16 years later.[14] Think about the financial freedom and flexibility those individuals have been given; the personal wealth each could have amassed from their early stock options. Beyond the ability to dedicate themselves to other non-financial pursuits, they could easily have pursued amazing professional opportunities elsewhere. For example, two of Google's largest competitors (Yahoo and AOL) are led today by CEOs who were recruited, at least in part, because of what they'd learned as early Google employees.

3. BE INTENTIONAL ABOUT WHO OWNS THE PROCESS . . . THE LEADERS!

Matt Mullenweg at Automattic spends at least one-third of his time on hiring. Specifically, he owns both the front end and final step of every candidate. On the front end, Matt is personally responsible for screening every resume that comes into Automattic. This allows him to direct those resumes to the right groups within the organization and also maintain a consistent standard for new recruits.[15] He also is the final step in every prospective candidate's interview process, doing an interview over instant messenger.[16]

While not involved as the screener, Reggie Aggarwal has maintained a very similar philosophy of being the final interviewer for all employees who are ultimately hired. He explained to *TechCrunch* that he has done this for over 800 Cvent employees "because I believe the basis of a successful company is good DNA."[17]

With over one million applicants at Google, Larry Page is not able to interview each candidate, but he does review every prospective candidate's hiring package before offers are extended. It's the last step in the interview process before offers are made and the package includes each interviewer's feedback, in addition to a candidate summary.[18]

4. CREATE A STRONG AND YET ADAPTIVE CULTURE

Once you've recruited and onboarded high performers, the next step is to create a culture that allows them to excel. Just as no one starts out with the goal of hiring dumb individuals, clearly most companies want employees to be engaged and contribute at their optimal level.

However, when it comes to engagement in most companies today, the statistics are sobering. Recent research by Gallup shows that nearly seven out of every ten employees are either not engaged or are actively disengaged at work today. Even at the executive and manager level it is still more than six out of ten.[19]

While we obviously weren't able to go back in time and run the same survey against our high-performing companies, it was clear from our secondary research that the individuals in our chosen companies applied amazing passion to their jobs and were very engaged.

As we sought for more clarity on each company's culture, we came across a group of academic researchers (Jennifer A. Chatman, David F. Caldwell, Charles A. O'Reilly, and Bernadette Doerr) from the University of California, Berkeley, Santa Clara University, and Stanford who have done significant research into the underlying culture of high-performing, high-growth companies.

For their research, they focused on the high-growth technology industry—specifically, 56 individual publicly traded tech companies, of which 89 percent were included in the Fortune 1000. These firms collectively represented 73 percent of the total 2009 revenues generated by technology-related Fortune 1000 companies. So, these companies are without a doubt some of the highest-performing companies in the world.[20]

Their hypothesis going into the research was that businesses with "strong cultures," which they defined as places in which "a high consensus exists among members across a broad set of culture norms," will have better financial performance even in rapidly changing and highly unstable environments.

At the conclusion of their research, after looking at company performance over a three-year period, they found that their hypothesis was correct—but they also added a second element of adaptability.

In terms of a strong culture, businesses that had a high consensus among employees on what the cultural norms of the organization both *should be* and *were,* and also had a high intensity in the belief of these organizational cultural norms, outperformed other businesses that were "characterized by lower consensus, lower intensity about adaptability, or both."[21]

PUTTING THIS INTO ACTION

Question 1: Have you built a great recruiting process (skill vs luck)?

In the earliest days of creating a company, many of the referrals you receive for new hires will come from people you know. Often the people referred are great candidates, but they need to go through a defined process just like everyone else.

There is a famous story about how Susan Wojcicki, a friend of Google's founders and the owner of the garage in which Google started, interviewed to be the first "business hire" of the company. She was put through the same process as any other candidate.[22] Susan has worked out well for Google, remains at the company today, and, after a very successful run as the person responsible for all commerce and advertising initiatives at Google, took over running YouTube after it was acquired by Google.

I don't advocate for this recruiting process simply because I enjoy rigidity, but because it allows you to apply a consistent filter to everyone. It helps you look back and discover whether the candidates who performed well were evaluated differently than those who didn't work out. This analysis can help you develop key interviewing skills and hone a great recruiting process, rather than hoping your hiring luck lasts.

Paul Otellini, the CEO of Intel and a board member at Google, once commented on the Google recruiting process to its leader of People Operations:

What's most impressive is that your team has built the world's first self-replicating talent machine. You've created a system that not only hires remarkable people, but also scales with the company and gets better with every generation.[23]

Question 2: Who owns the recruiting process?

I suspect most business leaders found themselves nodding along through the chapter. Very few leaders I talk to don't claim to place a priority on their people. Yet how many of these executives allocate material time to the process of recruiting great leaders?

In their book *How Google Works,* authors Eric Schmidt and Jonathan Rosenberg succinctly explain the need for strong recruiting practices: "Smart coaches know that no amount of strategy can substitute for talent, and that is as true in business as it is on the field. Scouting is like shaving: If you don't do it every day, it shows."[24]

Every day! Your calendar is a reflection of what you value and what you don't value. If you say you value hiring great people, but no one can get you to make time for it, you're shortchanging your own company.

Question 3: How does your process expose you to a candidate's real work?

While only Automattic, among the group of companies we studied, actually required all candidates to go through a process of trying out, all the firms we researched have their own systems, which reflect the qualities most crucial to their functioning. It is important that your process, whatever it is, try to estimate what the quality of a given candidate's contributions might be.

Even Google, a company notorious for its brain-teaser interviews, recently acknowledged that the interviews were not proving helpful in predicting employee success, and that they were shifting the process to focus more on the work that candidates had actually accomplished—what's called a structured behavioral interview.[25]

13

A CULTURE OF DISCIPLINE/FOCUS

"If you don't know where you're going, you'll end up somewhere else."

—Yogi Berra

YOU WOULD THINK THAT COMPANIES THAT ARE SCALING WOULD HAVE many more activities going on than those that never take off. However, looking across the case studies, we found the inverse to be true. There was a consistent pattern of successful companies staying focused on the few areas with the highest potential—to the point of proactively walking away from viable opportunities.

Put another way, "yes and . . ." is the enemy of growth. To elaborate, I suspect you've been in a meeting at which the goal going in was to prioritize and pick the highest-potential activities to focus on. Yet, in the end, the consensus seems to be to pick everything—or, at least, to choose more activities than you can reasonably tackle at any point in time.

The ability to be disciplined and maintain focus on the highest-priority goals was a true differentiator of the high-growth organizations we studied. In this chapter, we're going to focus on three specific pairs of companies: YouTube vs Revver, Facebook vs Friendster, and Tesla vs Fisker.

FACEBOOK'S FOCUS

Let's start at Facebook. Back in the mid-2000s, long before Facebook was on its way to generating huge revenues, everyone thought that Facebook was a cool product, but no one knew how it would ever make any money, and many skeptics suspected that it never would.

Anticipating this, even in the earliest days of Facebook's development, Noah Kagan, employee number 30 at Facebook, pitched Mark Zuckerberg with what he thought was a killer idea. Noah tried to persuade Mark that their next focus should be to prove the Facebook skeptics wrong and show them that the fledgling startup could make real money.

As Kagan recounts the story, Zuckerberg listened to the pitch and then:

> On a white board, he [Mark Zuckerberg] wrote the word "growth" and nothing else. He said if any feature didn't help do that then he was not interested and the idea was crushed. That was the only priority that mattered and his singular focus on accomplishing something has stuck with me till today. We had to do maintenance to the site, but all the big changes and things we worked towards were catching up and surpassing MySpace and taking over the world for connecting people. Singular focus—it helped us all stay on track, all the time.[1]

When you contrast this with Friendster at the same point in its history, the difference is stark. An article in the *New York Times,* doing a postmortem of Friendster, explained why:

> As Friendster became more popular, its overwhelmed Web site became slower. Things would become so bad that a Friendster Web page took as long as 40 seconds to download. Yet, from where Mr. Lindstrom sat, technical difficulties proved too pedestrian for a board of this pedigree. The performance problems would come up, but the board devoted most of its time to talking about potential competitors and new features, such as the possibility of adding Internet phone services, or so-called voice over Internet protocol, or VoIP, to the site.

The stars would never sit back and say, "We really have to make this thing work," recalled Mr. Lindstrom, who is now president of Friendster. "They were talking about the next thing. Voice over Internet. Making Friendster work in different languages. Potential big advertising deals. Yet we didn't solve the first basic problem: our site didn't work."[2]

It wasn't only Kent Lindstrom who thought that Friendster's lack of focus was a major issue. Jim Scheinman, one of the first employees at Friendster, did a post on the ten lessons he learned from Friendster. His first point is:

It's critical for a startup to have a clear focus, especially early on! Focus comes in many flavors. One key area of focus is product-focus. A start-up must choose what problem they are solving and stick to it until they've solved that problem, or it becomes clear that it's time to pivot. It was very difficult in the early days of Friendster to choose one direction and stay the course. Many smart investors, executives and team members all had great ideas on where to take this new thing called social networking.

Jim would go on to apply this and his other lessons in helping develop the social networking site Bebo, where he was the first employee, which was later sold to AOL for $850 million in 2008.[3]

I think this is a really important point. In both the cases of Noah pitching Mark and of the investors and executives pitching ideas for Friendster, the ideas themselves were "great," as Jim says. However, great ideas that aren't directly related to the most important mission of the company at the moment are not actually great. In a high-growth environment, you can only afford to focus on ideas that are both great and directly related to the highest priorities.

TESLA—TWO EXAMPLES

Elon Musk is a very smart and driven man. He has the unique ability to understand the root causes of a problem, and then formulate an elegant road map to the solutions for those problems. This is demonstrated by his numerous successes. More specifically, this can be seen in what he is doing with Tesla. Elon explains his approach as follows:

> My goal is to accelerate the advent of the electric car by whatever means necessary. And if we simply tried to sell electric powertrain technology to the car companies we would have had no success. We need to show by example.[4]

With this singular focus of accelerating the advent of the electric car, Elon understood that Tesla had to whittle down how it would accomplish this into a few key objectives, which were:

> The focus is on Tesla to ramp up the production rate, make sure quality's good, and then make sure . . . that the company's profitable. Because, obviously, there have been car company startups before that have brought cars into production. DeLorean and Tucker have done that, they built this debt, and then they died.[5]

Back in 2007, Elon realized that this focus was in jeopardy. The expected costs of production for the Tesla Roadster were unpalatable. The company would simply not survive without some damage control. So CEO Martin Eberhard, a co-founder of Tesla, was removed and replaced with Michael Marks.

Marks was the former CEO of the manufacturer Flextronics and an early Tesla investor. His chief qualification for the position of CEO was that during his 13-year tenure with Flextronics he expanded the company into 35 countries, made 100 acquisitions, and substantially grew revenue from $93 million to $16 billion.[6]

As Marks describes it, "When I got there, the economics, the business structure were terrible. If it wasn't terrible, they wouldn't have brought me in."[7] To illustrate how bad things were when Marks arrived, he immediately had to set about killing a $30 million order for car parts that were about to be shipped to Tesla, despite the fact Tesla hadn't even finished the design of the car. In addition, before Marks's arrival, Tesla had begun doing R&D for other companies, but still had not produced a single Tesla car. Marks saw that Tesla was losing focus on the idea that it had to lead by example in the electric car industry. Before branching out, the company had to first create an amazing electric car that consumers wanted. The R&D for other companies was eliminated from Tesla's activities.

The biggest contribution that Marks might have made in helping Tesla crawl out of the grave is what has come to be known as "Marks's List." "Marks's List" emerged when Marks met with all the executives and created a list of things that needed to be done before Tesla's first production car was ready to be shipped. This list was only 30 items long! Can you imagine how many things go into producing a car? And Marks was able to take all the elements needed to make the world's greatest electric vehicle and turn them into a list of just 30 items!

Marks assigned each of these 30 items to someone on the executive team, and then held regular meetings to ensure that the person who had been assigned that task was making sufficient progress.

Marks was a very good CEO. He understood that his role was to ensure the company stayed focused on accomplishing its vision, and to eliminate or change anything that did not align with Tesla's vision.

YOUTUBE ANTI-EXAMPLE: REVVER

Chances are you've never heard of Revver. Revver was an upstart competitor to YouTube, and its ideas about the future of online video were 100 percent correct. So why have most people never heard of the company? Well, because it had ideas, rather than just ONE idea.

As Ian Clarke, co-founder of Revver, explained in a Quora post:

> Revver was way too ambitious. With a relatively small amount of funding, we were trying to build a video sharing network, build a video ad network, all while doing our best to obey all of the laws that our competitors were studiously ignoring at the time. Recall that YouTube achieved much of its early growth off the back of an SNL skit called "Lazy Sunday"— which they [NBC] wouldn't allow today. In short, we were trying to build 2014's YouTube back in 2006.[8]

The lesson? Revver should have focused on building a video-sharing network. The path to profit could emerge after capturing users with an undeniably great video-sharing network. This was made obvious by YouTube's success.

YouTube set out to do one thing, and that was to make it simple for anyone in the world to upload, view, and share videos. That's it. The company wasn't distracted by how to monetize this platform or even by questions of copyright infringement; it was only worried about making it irresistibly easy to upload, share, and view videos. Chad Hurley, one of YouTube's founders, credited the lack of a revenue-sharing model as one of the reasons for YouTube's success because, according to a BBC report, it "allowed the website to focus on its key strength, making it easy to share videos with others."[9]

The company knew that if it could achieve this key goal of making it easy to share videos with others, its chances of becoming wildly popular would be better than those of its competitors. YouTube also knew that if it became wildly successful, then dealing with the other issues, such as copyright infringement, would become much easier and clearer.

This became clear when "Lazy Sunday" propelled YouTube into the spotlight and brought out the issue of copyright infringement. Rather than end terribly for YouTube, its facilitation of copyright infringement of NBC's material turned into a mutually beneficial deal with NBC. NBC at first asked YouTube to take the material down, but when the network saw that SNL ratings went up after "Lazy Sunday" went viral with over 7 million views, and when it considered the struggle the music industry was dealing with at the hands of Napster, it quickly realized that rather than trying to beat YouTube, the network should team up with it.[10]

PUTTING THIS INTO ACTION

Question 1: How do your activities map to your vision?

We talked about the importance of vision throughout the first section of this book (prerequisites). I don't want to repeat all of that here, but the key point, as we said at the start of this chapter, is that if you don't know where you are going, it's impossible to get to where you want to go.

As you start thinking about putting this into action, the first step is to remind yourself and your team where you are striving to end up.

Question 2: What are the important goals for the company as they relate to that vision?

Once you've clarified that vision. The next step is to make it clear to yourself and the rest of your team what is truly important to focus on and by extension what is not important.

It's easy to slip into a routine of working really hard without getting the most important things done. We do busy work, such as trying to reach in-box zero or take one more coffee meeting to be polite, instead of doing the things that advance our key priorities and long-term goals.

Why is it so difficult to put this obviously good advice into practice? Upon waking up in the morning, most of us get bombarded by notifications from our phones, computers, and tablets. These clamoring demands compete for our limited attention, threatening to pull us in a hundred different directions. The first step to working intelligently is to rise above the noise and decide what NOT to do.

As Steve Jobs famously quipped: "Deciding what NOT to do is as important as deciding what to do."

One simple way to determine what NOT to do is to use a method I first learned from Stephen Covey's *Seven Habits of Highly Effective People*.[11] I recently discovered[12] that the method was actually pioneered by former President Dwight D. Eisenhower.

As you may recall from history class, Eisenhower was an amazingly productive leader. In addition to serving as president of the United States in the 1950s, Ike was a five-star general who led Allied forces during WWII. During his tenure as president, he spearheaded the creation of the interstate highway system, DARPA (Al Gore has him to thank for the Internet), and NASA.

To optimize his time, Eisenhower created a simple matrix divided into four boxes with the following categories:

1. Urgent and important (tasks you will do immediately).
2. Important, but not urgent (tasks you will schedule to do later).
3. Urgent, but not important (tasks you will try to delegate to someone else).
4. Neither urgent nor important (tasks that you will eliminate).

Here's what the Eisenhower box would look like:

Figure 13.1—Eisenhower's Matrix

	URGENT	NOT URGENT
IMPORTANT	Do	Plan
NOT IMPORTANT	Delegate	Eliminate

Coming back to your vision, as defined in Step 1, the key thing this matrix can help you determine is what is urgent vs important, which helps you to stop reacting to tasks (activities) and start focusing on what advances your long-term goals (results)!

> What is important is seldom urgent and what is urgent is seldom important.
>
> Dwight Eisenhower

Question 3: How are you empowering your employees to focus on their goals?

In order to empower his employees to focus on company goals, Peter Thiel—founder of PayPal, highly successful investor, and author of *Zero to One*—created a philosophy of management that he calls "one thing." According to PayPal executive Keith Rabois, Thiel "would refuse to discuss virtually anything else with you except what was currently assigned as your #1 initiative." In addition, Thiel would require employees to identify their single most valuable contribution to the company during their annual reviews.[13]

Rabois further explained:

The most important benefit of this approach is that it impels the organization to solve the challenges with the highest impact. Without this discipline, there is a consistent tendency of employees to address the easier to conquer, albeit less valuable, imperatives. As a specific example, if you have 3 priorities and the most difficult one lacks a clear solution, most people will gravitate towards the 2nd order task with a clearer path to an answer.

As a result, the organization collectively performs at a B+ or A– level, but misses many of the opportunities for a step-function in value creation.[14]

While you may not need a method as extreme as that used by Thiel at PayPal, there is no doubt that you need to keep your employees focused, and that in trying to do this your primary job will be to remove distractions and obstacles (this includes yourself).

Besides helping to focus your team on what needs to be done, you've also got to remove distractions that prevent them from focusing on their work. This is especially important as your organization grows. As Airbnb's CTO Mike Curtis explains, "as size and complexity of an organization increases, productivity of individuals working in that organization tends to decrease." This decrease in output is usually the result of too many policies and their accompanying paperwork getting in the way. Rather than creating more and more policies as your organization grows, Curtis encourages the reduction of rules through a tactic he calls "replacing policy with principles."

So what does replacing policy with principles look like? Well, one example from Airbnb involves its expense reporting system. The old policy was that all expenses required pre-approval. Any charge, regardless of size, would need to be approved before being submitted. As Curtis says, "I can't tell you how much pain in my life has come from expense reports."

So Curtis came up with a new principle, which was "if you would think twice about spending this much from your own account, gut check it with your manager." To aid in this principle, $500 was set up as a rule of thumb for when to get a gut-check. With this new principle in place, tons of time was saved, and there was also no increase in discretionary spending.

With a change as simple as that, Curtis was able to save time (and therefore money) for Airbnb. He recognized that if you've hired the right people, you should be able to trust their judgment. If you can't, you probably need to look into improving your hiring practices.[15]

ANTI-EXAMPLE, JUNO

Juno didn't share this same faith in its employees. Joel Spolsky is a software developer and entrepreneur in New York City who writes influential essays on software development philosophy at his blog *Joel on Software.* Earlier in his career Joel worked for (and then left) Juno; from a post he wrote in March of 2000, it's clear that it was not a satisfying part of his work history. After talking about a particularly frustrating experience at Juno, he explained that the culture was such that:

> [N]o matter how hard you work, no matter how smart you are, no matter whether you are "in charge" of something or not, you have no authority whatsoever for even the tiniest thing. None. Take your damn ideas, training, brains, and intelligence, all the things we're paying you for, and shove it.[16]

Question 4: Are you spending time understanding what did and didn't work?

Finally, it's not enough to simply have your employees focused on the highest-priority items. It's important to understand, in hindsight, what did and did not work. As you understand this more concretely, you can continue to improve and move faster.

One technique that a lot of companies (including many in our study) use today to manage their engineering process is Scrum. Scrum is a project management framework that was originally designed for software development, but works well for any complex and innovative projects.

One of the six key principles of Scrum is:

> At the end of each sprint there should be a retrospective, that is a review of what went well, what went poorly, and what improvements to the process can be made. The review should be done as soon as possible after the completion of the sprint. This way the sprint is still fresh in everyone's minds. The retrospective should also seek to identify specific things the team should start doing, stop doing, and continue doing.[17]

While the method to Scrum is pretty easy, putting it into action requires discipline, and a team that wants to be the best. Jeff Sutherland, one of the originators of Scrum, said that when he was formulating the Scrum methodology he used a rule (borrowed originally from the MIT Media Lab) he called "demo or die," which meant that during a monthlong sprint, he expected his software development team to demo new features that were being worked on weekly and get feedback on them. Although the team resisted this, he encouraged them to continue the practice. Over time, beyond simply providing a goal for each sprint, this also allowed the team to spend time talking about how to improve their process on a regular basis.[18]

Whether you use Scrum or not, rapid feedback is critical to being able to understand what is and is not working for your team. It allows you to make changes to the process on the fly rather than waiting for the entire project to come to a grinding halt.

14

MAXIMIZING THE VALUE OF NETWORK

"All big successes in the Internet Century will embody large platforms that get better and stronger as they grow."

—Eric Schmidt and Jonathan Rosenberg[1]

THE FIRST TIME I TAUGHT THE SCIENCE OF GROWTH AS A COURSE AT CARnegie Mellon, my teaching assistant, Matt Crespi, and I had planned that he would give a short lecture on network effects. It's his area of academic focus, and both of us found ourselves repeatedly frustrated by the misuse of the term "network effects" in earlier entrepreneurship courses we had taught together. It felt like a great opportunity to clarify what is and what is not a network effect.

As we spent more time discussing the material and looking over examples, we realized a short lecture would not be sufficient and ended up dedicating an entire evening to the material, which was extremely well received. We came to believe that thinking through ways to amplify and strengthen emerging networks is critical to long-term scalable success for most businesses.

We aren't alone in this belief. According to Matt Buchanan of Giz-modo.com, Mark Zuckerberg at Facebook has been aware of the power of network effects for years. In an article written the day before Facebook went public in 2012, Matt described his first meeting with Zuckerberg in 2007:

> [I]t was clear he'd [Zuckerberg] already become a student of what made entrepreneurs like Bill Gates at Microsoft, and Larry Page and Sergey Brin at Google so successful. They all created businesses with powerful network effects—businesses, as Zuckerberg explained it to me, that at a certain point attracted new users simply so they could interact with exist-ing users. "I think that network effects shouldn't be underestimated with what we do as well," he said.[2]

At its core, a business with a network effect is one in which the value of the solution increases as more customers take advantage of it. The first example most people point to when discussing network effects is the telephone. The value of all telephones increases as each additional person owns one.

However, over the last few decades, technology has created products with similar dynamics to the telephone. As noted earlier, Bob Metcalfe, in-ventor of Ethernet (core technology enabling most computers to be con-nected via networks) and co-founder of the company 3Com, proposed "Metcalfe's Law" to quantify these dynamics. The law dictates that the value of a network increases proportionately with the square of the number of its compatibly communicating devices. Bob proposed this "law" to get compa-nies to install local networks and connect their computers together so they could share files and communicate across the company. A dozen years later, the "law" was reframed to talk about connected "users" vs "compatible com-munication devices," and today most people define Metcalfe's Law as the "value of a network is the number of users squared."[3]

Over the last few decades, entire companies were built on leveraging the Internet to connect individuals to each other. Of the companies we studied, both Facebook and LinkedIn are businesses in which the core product is a network of individual connections. In such cases, your friends or profes-sional connections form the network, and as you add additional connec-tions, the service becomes more valuable.

Networks are, at their most basic, made up of "nodes," which, in the case of Facebook or LinkedIn, are people, and the relationships between nodes, which are called "edges." Nodes in non-social networks can be things like companies, cities, or airports, and the edges can be things like trading partnerships, cables, and flight paths.

PayPal is another business with a classic network effect. The value of the network increased as more people used it. This is because, in order to send or receive money, you needed a PayPal account. PayPal is worthless if you're the only person you know with an account, because then you can't take advantage of its value proposition. However, as more and more people sign up for PayPal the value starts to scale because there are more and more people who could *potentially* use the network to send money. In a network, it's not just the number of nodes but the number of *potential ties* (or connections) that provides the utility.

The case of PayPal touches on another important concept from network theory—bipartite networks. In this type of network, there are two different types of nodes. For PayPal, this would be people sending money and those receiving it. Obviously, many PayPal customers have done both in their time using the service, but if everyone was only interested in sending money (or only interested in receiving it) the network would not have any value.

In other bipartite networks, the types of nodes are distinct. Of the companies we studied, Tumblr and Twitter both ended up building a network of people connecting to each other, while leveraging the content those people created as another node. *Wired* magazine explained how Tumblr built its network:

> Tumblr is extremely easy to use as a free-form blogging platform, but has also developed into its own social network. Users follow other tumblelogs, whose content appears in their dashboards, not unlike Facebook's newsfeed; hitting the "reblog" button publishes that post to their own blogs, a feature Tumblr put out two years before Twitter introduced its own retweet button. "The social network that emerges out of Tumblr is interesting because it's driven by content, not by the social graph that these other networks are building around," says John Maloney, the company's

president. And that content spreads quickly: on average, a Tumblr post gets reblogged nine times.[4]

One specific type of bipartite network that is very common and increasingly important is the two-sided marketplace. In this case, a company aggregates two large networks, broadly referred to as suppliers and consumers, and acts as the intermediary joining them together. For example, as you look at our chosen companies, think of Uber connecting people needing a ride with drivers and Airbnb connecting travelers with people looking to rent out spare space in (or even the entirety of) their homes.

No investor may have more experience with two-sided marketplaces than Bill Gurley, a partner at Benchmark Capital. His firm has been involved in several successful marketplace businesses such as eBay, OpenTable, Yelp, Zillow, oDesk, and Uber. As Bill explained a few years ago, first the Internet and now mobile devices have made it easier to create these types of marketplaces:

> Entrepreneurs accurately recognize that the connective tissue of the Internet provides an opportunity to link the players in a particular market, reducing friction in both the buying and selling experience. The arrival of the smartphone amplifies these opportunities, as the Internet's connective tissue now extends deeper and deeper into an industry with the participants connected to the marketplace 24×7—whether they are in the office, at home, or out in the field.

He added that a critical point about these types of businesses is that both the supplier and consumer side of the marketplace need to demonstrate network effects:

> A true marketplace needs natural pull on both the consumer and supplier side of the market. Aggregating suppliers is a necessary, but insufficient step on its own. You must also organically aggregate demand. With each step, it should get easier to acquire the incremental consumer AS WELL AS the incremental supplier. Highly liquid marketplaces naturally "tip" towards becoming a clearinghouse where neither the consumer nor the

supplier would favor an alternative. That only happens if your momentum is increasing, and both consumers and suppliers are sensing an increasing importance of your place in the world. Much easier said than done.[5]

Up to this point in the chapter, each example given is what is known as a direct network effect. In such cases, every node benefits from the addition of additional connected nodes on the network. Or put another way, with a direct network effect increased usage of the product *directly* leads to an increase in value of the solution. Therefore, every node is at least implicitly motivated to increase adoption of the overall network.

There is a second type of network effect, which is still very important—indirect network effect. An indirect network is created when the adoption of a product causes an effect on a separate but related market. You can think of an indirect network effect as one in which the increase in value is really a *byproduct* of so many customers taking advantage of a solution.

Let's continue thinking about two-sided marketplaces, but now think about creating them via *indirect network effects.* In the case of Google, the company had millions of people using its search product to find what they were looking for on the Internet. Google recognized it had a huge captive audience and realized advertisers would like to connect with this audience based on audience interests. As Google connected advertisers to consumers, both Google and the advertisers ended up benefiting from the adoption of the product by the other network. Advertisers supported the company financially, making it viable for Google to improve its core offering and create additional services. Advertisers benefited from these improvements as additional consumers spent more of their attention within the Google ecosystem, allowing the advertisers more opportunities to reach them.

Cvent provides another example of an indirect network effect. In 2008, Cvent supported over 10,000 clients in over 90 countries through its online solution, allowing users across the world to more efficiently plan their hundreds of thousands of events. After investing two years and over $10 million, the company introduced the Cvent Supplier Network, a marketplace to connect its customers—the event planners—with suppliers whose services they might use, specifically focusing on hotels, restaurants, and special event venues. It's worth pointing out that when Cvent added this functionality, it was not a small company. It not only had over 10,000 customers, it also had over 1,400 employees and was profitable enough to invest $10 million in the creation of the new product.[6]

However, the Cvent Supplier Network (CSN) today is a meaningful part of the business. From the most recent annual report:

> The number of event requests for proposal, or RFPs, submitted through our marketplace has increased from approximately 12,000 in 2008, the year CSN was initiated, to approximately 1.6 million in 2014. As a result of this substantial growth, we believe we have achieved critical mass and are benefiting from substantial network effects as increased adoption of our marketplace by planners attracts hoteliers to leverage our growing event planner user base to expand their group business activity.

Later in the same annual report, the company explained that these marketing solutions represent 30 percent of its total revenue, $42 million of the $142 million earned in 2014.[7]

An indirect network effect can sometimes occur even when the core product offering is already driven by a direct network effect. For example, LinkedIn and Facebook have both created a marketplace of advertisers they use to connect with individuals using their platforms.

In other cases, a company may start out leveraging an existing network but later develop its own network. As discussed in Chapter 7, YouTube derived a lot of its initial growth drafting off the social network MySpace. However, in August of 2006 YouTube surpassed MySpace in popularity. What's interesting is that over the last few years YouTube has introduced features to increase the connectivity between content creators and fans, causing some analysts to consider it one of the largest social networks in the US.[8]

In many ways, Facebook's introduction of people nodes in addition to content nodes is similar to approaches taken by Tumblr and Twitter. However, unlike the early bipartite network examples, YouTube came to this later, after it had already developed a content network that leveraged pre-existing social networks, especially MySpace.

Indirect network effects are important because most products deliver value without a network effect. However, you can often introduce an indirect network effect as you're scaling, to amplify value. If you're trying to grow a company, pay attention to the networks—and potential networks—at play.

Tesla provides an interesting example of this, creating indirect network effects with its Supercharger stations. For those not familiar with the stations, in 2012 Tesla introduced these Supercharger stations to provide Model S owners with free access to a special charger that would allow owners to fully charge their electric car in an hour. The chargers only work with Model S cars and many are solar-powered.[9] While Tesla originally introduced just six chargers, exclusively in California, the Supercharger networks are now so widespread that Tesla owners can drive across the country from California to New England, relying completely on Superchargers.[10]

For many people, the big objection to owning an electric car is their anxiety that they'll one day find themselves driving and realize that not only do they not have enough battery life to make it to their destination, but there is nowhere for them to charge the car, leaving them to sadly drive past gas station after gas station until their battery finally runs down and they need to call a tow truck. The folks at Tesla call this "range anxiety."

The Supercharger network helps eliminate this range anxiety, making it more attractive to own an electric car (specifically Tesla's electric car, since the charger only works with Model S vehicles). While hard to quantify, since you can't extrapolate how many purchases over the last few years would have occurred with or without the network, the increase in charging stations will theoretically lead to an increase in demand for Tesla's cars, since an obvious pain point has now been eliminated.

PUTTING THIS INTO ACTION

Question 1: Are there existing direct network effects in your business you can strengthen?

If a key part of your value comes from connections and potential connections, as was the case for Facebook, LinkedIn, PayPal, and Airbnb, then you need to ask yourself what you can do to strengthen those connections. It may be as simple as introducing new features, like LinkedIn's introduction of PYMK (from Chapter 10), or, if your business isn't a software company, you might add features or functionality in a more concrete way.

A familiar example of this comes from wireless carriers. The carriers have technological networks, but since all phones need to be able to call all other phones, it's the technology rather than the carriers that gets those network effects. However, cell phone companies still try to find ways to allow meaningful person-to-person ties on their networks (for example, Verizon offering free customer-to-customer calling that doesn't eat into your minutes).

Question 2: Are there indirect network effects you should create or strengthen?

Consider the Tesla example: There are plenty of people who purchased Teslas before the first Supercharging station was constructed; however, by adding the charging stations, Tesla was able to introduce an indirect network effect and make owning a Tesla car more valuable.

Question 3: Are you able to take a group of your customers and increase their aggregate value with a marketplace?

In many cases, as you start to aggregate customers who get value from your core product, there is an opportunity to leverage the fact you have an engaged group of individuals by connecting them with other businesses that might have trouble getting their attention. Earlier in the chapter, I discussed how Google and its advertisers used this technique to try to reach you and all of your friends, but also discussed the more nuanced example of Cvent, which added a supplier network to its existing group of event planners.

15

CONCLUSION

IF YOU'RE IN THE MIDDLE OF LAUNCHING AN INNOVATIVE PRODUCT, either as an intrapreneur or entrepreneur, I know without even meeting you that you have more items competing for your time than you could possibly accomplish every day. The last thing I want to do is add more to your to-do list. Instead, I hope you'll come away from this book with a new set of tools and best practices that can help you "dent the universe," as Steve Jobs famously said, and make sure your product or service has the impact that you hoped for.

I would recommend you start really assessing where you are in the progression of commercializing your innovation. Are you somewhere along the path to satisfying the four prerequisites discussed in the first section of this book? If so, make sure you progress through those to avoid scaling prematurely.

If, on the other hand, you truly have satisfied each of the four prerequisites, is the problem now that not enough people are aware of your solution? Think through the different catalysts we discussed in the second section, and figure out which of these might amplify the awareness of your product or service.

Finally, are you growing quickly? Then transition to focusing on the foundation of your business to ensure long-term growth, as discussed in the third section of this book. A brittle foundation in any of these principles will make it challenging to maintain long-term sustainable scaling growth.

DON'T REST ON SUCCESS

Finally, it's important to point out that we've been very focused on the early years in the development of the companies we studied—*after* they had already built a product their target customers care about, and were experiencing rapid growth. The success and scale that each achieved did not eliminate the need to continue to innovate. Some of the companies from our list seem to be doing a better job than others at remaining innovative. This is an important topic, but it is one we have not focused on, in any detail, in this book.

All new employees at Facebook get what they refer to as *Facebook's Little Red Book*. It's a way to communicate the history, mission, and values of the company. One of the last pages of that book says:

> If we don't create the thing that kills Facebook, someone else will.
>
> "Embracing change" isn't enough. It has to be so hardwired into who we are that even talking about it seems redundant. The Internet is not a friendly place. Things that don't stay relevant don't even get the luxury of leaving ruins. They disappear.[1]

Perhaps the most obvious example of this risk from among the companies we studied is the case of Hotmail after its acquisition by Microsoft. At the time of its acquisition Hotmail was the dominant email provider. Yet it didn't maintain that market lead, and in 2004, Google released Gmail, which, eight years later, became the largest web-based email solution, surpassing 425 million active users.[2]

What's interesting is that Gmail used a lot of the same techniques attributed to Hotmail and other selected companies earlier in this book. The following section maps Gmail's success within the framework we have discussed throughout this book.

First, let's review the four prerequisites that you need to satisfy before scaling.

Prerequisite 1—Founder's Core Vision: It turns out Google's Paul Buchheit had been passionate about web-based email solutions long before he joined the company. In fact, in 1996, he started working on a side project to deliver web-based email, predating even Hotmail. Then, years later, as Google's 23rd employee, assigned to the Google Groups project, he convinced his management to allow him to refocus the company's efforts on his old passion.[3]

After Gmail succeeded, Paul left Google and co-founded FriendFeed—which was ultimately acquired by Facebook—and most recently joined Y Combinator as a partner.[4]

Prerequisite 2—Scalable Idea: Certainly, finding a significantly better approach to email is a big idea. The challenge inside Google was to convince people that the company should be doing anything beyond operating as a search engine. While today Google does all kinds of interesting projects, Gmail was its first foray outside of web search.

Prerequisite 3—Solves a Real Problem: There are a few things I'd point out here.

First, the "goodness factor" for Gmail came primarily from the ability to efficiently search email. This was its original feature. In an interview with founding partner at Y Combinator Jessica Livingston in her book *Founders at Work,* Paul pointed out that at Google there was a very email-intense culture; he alone received 500 emails per day. So, to him and to the co-workers to whom he initially released the product, an efficient way to search through email was revolutionary.

The other goodness factor was the sheer amount of space that Google was providing—a gigabyte of space. For perspective, most of the other email clients provided two to four megabytes, so this was literally 250 to 500 times as much space.

The other thing to point out is that while Google later launched the product to the public (which we'll describe below), it had received lots of feedback before the launch. As Paul explained to Jessica in that same interview, the company was constantly getting validation that customers liked the product they were building:

> Literally from day one, we had users internally. One nice thing about Google is that we can just release things internally and have this great population of testers, essentially. So people inside have been using Gmail from a long time [when it launched.][5]

Prerequisite 4—An Excellent First Interaction: The Gmail team was very focused on getting the perspectives of those internal users on what was frustrating and what could be enhanced. From the same interview:

> Livingston: It sounds like you really took the user's perspective when you designed Gmail.
>
> Buchheit: Absolutely, that's very much how it developed. Every time we would get irritated by some little problem, or one of the users would say, "I have this problem, it isn't working for me," we'd just spend time thinking about it, looking at what the underlying problems are and how we can come up with a solution to make it better for them.[6]

As you may recall, in April of 2004, when Google introduced Gmail to the general public, it actually restricted invitations to the service. It turns out this was more of a product constraint than anything. Given the fact that every user was getting one gigabyte of email storage, coupled with the restrictions on how many servers were used to deploy the solution, these restrictions allowed Google to guarantee a great product experience.

While many assume this was simply a marketing ploy, even now Paul seems honestly frustrated with the slow rollout of invitations even though his commitment to the constraint created a great first experience. Commenting to *Time* magazine on Google's tenth anniversary he explained: "I think Gmail could have grown a lot more in the first year if we'd had more resources."[7]

Whether you think users bidding for invites on eBay was a good or bad thing, limiting invites was an important constraint the team embraced to ensure a great interaction for the customers who were on the product.

As I've looked at the Gmail case, it seems they used two of the four catalysts to really accelerate their growth:

Catalyst 1: Double Trigger Events

While most people remember the limited number of invitations for Gmail, what fewer remember years later is that the service was first introduced on April 1. Google had a long history of embracing April Fools' jokes, and the company decided that since the idea of one gigabyte of free storage sounded so crazy, they'd go along with this and launch the service on April 1.[8]

It worked: When Google told the media about the service, the media couldn't decide whether this was real or the most elaborate April Fools' joke ever. The team at Google even used humor in its press release to feed this speculation, including quotes like:

Search is Number Two Online Activity—Email is Number One; "Heck, Yeah," Say Google Founders . . . The inspiration for Gmail came from a Google user complaining about the poor quality of existing email services, recalled Larry Page, Google co-founder and president, Products. "She kvetched about spending all her time filing messages or trying to find them . . ." "If a Google user has a problem with email, well, so do we," said Google co-founder and president of technology, Sergey Brin. "And while developing Gmail was a bit more complicated than we anticipated, we're pleased to be able to offer it to the user who asked for it."[9]

While the team at Google, even back in 2004, didn't have trouble getting media coverage for their initiatives, the April 1 release date did add to the story. Journalist and discussion forums like Slashdot weren't sure if the idea was real or an elaborate prank, and some even went so far as to speculate that it was an April Fools' joke, but it was now getting more publicity than Google could have possibly wanted.

Catalyst 2: Viral Growth

Coming back to the product constraints, I certainly understand Paul's argument above that opening the service up faster would have added more users to the email service the first year. However, I do think the fact that customers were able to extend invitations to other potential customers certainly helped turn their customers into advocates. Obviously, there is no way to go back and know how much this invitation system contributed to or constrained early growth. As *Time* magazine explained in the ten-year anniversary story mentioned earlier:

> Bidding for invites on eBay sent prices shooting up to $150 and beyond; sites such as Gmail Swap emerged to match up those with invites with those who desperately wanted them. Having a Hotmail or Yahoo Mail email address was slightly embarrassing; having a Gmail one meant that you were part of a club most people couldn't get into.[10]

It was exactly this club-like feeling of a Gmail address that allowed Google to turn its customers into advocates. What started as a technical constraint to create a great first interaction ended up reinforcing a powerful catalyst: getting customers to recruit more customers.

The Gmail team was able to leverage a lot of the same foundational elements as Google's first successful product (search). There are a few things that I think are really interesting and worth pointing out.

In terms of financing growth appropriately, the Gmail team had an advantage: Unlike most startups, the team didn't have to raise capital from outside investors, but instead had to win the support of the leadership team at Google. While this is a different sales process than putting pitch decks together for feedback from VCs, it is still an important part of the process. When I talk to intrapreneurs at large companies who want to do big things, they often seem frustrated at the process of procuring resources. But getting resources is part of the process and something that can't be overlooked, no matter how tempting.

The other element I wanted to call out was how strategic Gmail was in maximizing the value of its network. It's interesting to me that immediately before coming to Gmail, Paul was part of the Google Groups team. Google leveraged its significantly better email solution (500x goodness factor at the time) to build strong networks. Specifically, the company has used that single authentication to provide numerous other solutions, including its office productivity suite, and to increase the percentage of people who use its search tool as a logged-in experience so the company can personalize the results.

Google now calls all of its super-ambitious projects—moonshots. This includes everything from self-driving cars, to Google Glass, to providing Internet connectivity via blimps, to many things that I'm sure they are working on that we haven't even heard about yet. In the foreword to *How Google Works* by Eric Schmidt and Jonathan Rosenberg, Larry Page commented:

> Over time I've learned, surprisingly, that it's tremendously hard to get teams to be super ambitious. It turns out most people haven't been educated in this kind of moonshot thinking. They tend to assume that things are impossible, rather than starting from real-world physics and figuring out what's actually possible. It's why we've put so much energy into hiring independent thinkers at Google, and setting big goals. Because if you hire the right people and have big enough dreams, you'll usually get there. And even if you fail, you'll probably learn something important.[11]

I think that's the best note to end on. I hope these stories have inspired you to think big, provided a framework to think about the process to do this, and ultimately increased your chance to succeed. Innovation is hard, but it's one of the most rewarding things you can do. Now please go create products and services that make the world the way it ought to be.

APPENDIX

COMPANY OVERVIEWS

THE GOAL OF THIS APPENDIX IS TO PROVIDE AN OVERVIEW OF EACH OF THE PAIRS OF companies we studied. This should provide helpful background for understanding the illustrations through the rest of this book.

The pairs are reviewed in reverse-chronological order, beginning with the companies that started up most recently (Tumblr vs Posterous) and ending with the oldest of the paired companies (McDonald's vs White Castle).

Unless otherwise noted, I will only include capital provided by venture rounds and not secondary financings or debt financings. I do my best to responsibly delineate between different financing events but would be the first to point out that the market is ambiguous these days.

TUMBLR VS POSTEROUS
Product Overview

Tumblr and Posterous were designed to be simpler versions of full-scale blogging platforms like WordPress and Movable Type (described below). These platforms, sometimes described as "microblogs," focused primarily on shorter—and often more visual—content like videos and pictures.

The first example of this type of site was created by Chris Neukirchen, a 17-year-old German who wrote the code for his site himself in March of 2005. Two years later Chris heard from David Karp, who said he was launching his own project, called Tumblr, inspired by Chris's idea.[1] A year later, Posterous entered the startup accelerator Y Combinator and launched a competing project.

Financing[2]

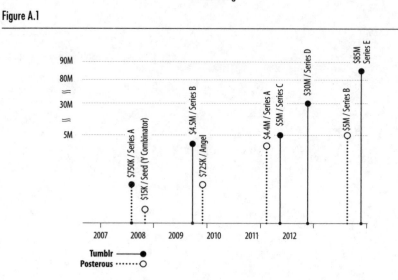

Leadership Team

Tumblr was founded by David Karp. While David never attended college and, after transitioning to being homeschooled, never even finished high school, he did have an interesting set of work experiences at a young age. Specifically, he was the chief technology officer (CTO) of UrbanBaby until it was sold to CNET in 2006 and earlier in his career interned for the media creative and animation producer Fred Seibert.[3] He started Tumblr when he was 20 years old.

Marco Arment was not technically Tumblr's founder but he was the first employee and a critical "partner" with David during the platform's development. Marco was the CTO and Lead Developer of Tumblr from its inception until he left to focus full-time on a side project—Instapaper.

David and Marco originally started working together in the consulting firm David started after cashing out his equity from the sale of UrbanBaby. When David and Marco had a gap in client projects, they spent a few weeks working on creating Tumblr.

Posterous was started by Sachin Agarwal, Garry Tan, and Brett Gibson. Sachin started his career at Apple as an engineer and according to his LinkedIn profile: "Started Posterous on my couch in New York City. Built the first version myself as a way to post photos from my iPhone to my blog."[4] He was joined by Garry Tan, who had worked as a program manager at Microsoft and also as an engineer and designer at the software company Palantir.[5]

Customer Traction

For both Tumblr and Posterous, the initial business strategy was to create a large network of content creators who would publish on their services. In the early years, they prioritized this ahead of monetizing the audience. Once successful, Tumblr was able to introduce advertising on its network as the primary revenue model. Yahoo (the company that ultimately acquired Tumblr) projected on its October 2014 earnings call that Tumblr would be doing over $100 million in revenue and would be profitable in 2015.[6] However, in the early years the relevant traction metrics were not revenue, but the number of microblogs created on the platform and how popular those sites were with their audiences (which, in aggregate, formed Tumblr's audience).

Number of Microblogs Created[7]

TABLE A.1

	Tumblr	Posterous
2007	170,000	n/a
2008	1,000,000	n/a
2009	2,000,000	125,000
2010	7,000,000	4,000,000
2011	38,000,000	12,000,000

Exit

Tumblr was acquired for $1.1 billion in 2013 by Yahoo. At the time this was the highest acquisition price paid for a social networking company, surpassing the previous record set by Facebook's acquisition of Instagram.[8] At the time of the announcement of the acquisition, Yahoo CEO Marissa Mayer justified the price, explaining:

> Tumblr has built an amazing place to follow the world's creators. From art to architecture, fashion to food, Tumblr hosts 105 million different blogs. With more than 300 million monthly unique visitors and 120,000 signups every day, Tumblr is one of the fastest-growing media networks in the world. Tumblr sees 900 posts per second (!) and 24 billion minutes spent onsite each month . . . The combination of Tumblr+Yahoo! could grow Yahoo!'s audience by 50% to more than a billion monthly visitors, and could grow traffic by approximately 20%.[9]

While the terms of the Posterous acquisition were not disclosed, it was largely believed to be what is known in Silicon Valley as an "acqui-hire" in which the ultimate value of the acquisition is the talented team (typically engineers) that the acquiring company gets along with the business. This supposition was validated when Twitter shut down the Posterous service a year after completing the acquisition.[10] The most credible rumors were that Twitter paid a $5 million to $10 million acquisition price.

TESLA VS FISKER

Product Overview

Tesla and Fisker both created a luxury electric car, but took very different approaches to its design and development. While there had been attempts to create both hybrid vehicles and fully electric vehicles before, the efforts made by these two startups to create a premium vehicle to attract a significant portion of the luxury market were the most significant.

The first product created by Tesla was the Roadster. The body (or what is called a "glider" in the industry) was purchased from the English car company Lotus, which used the same shell for producing its Lotus Elise sports car. Once Tesla sold out of the 2,400 gliders it had contracted from Lotus it transitioned its sales and development efforts toward the Tesla Model S sedan.[11]

Financing[12]

Figure A.2

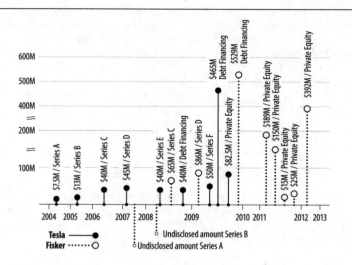

Leadership Team

Although many people believe that Elon Musk founded Tesla, that is actually not the case. Instead, Elon originally led the Series A investment. It was only later, after the original founder moved on and after a short period with an interim CEO, that Elon took over responsibility as the CEO. With that said, it's hard to overstate the importance of his role in the company. Even before becoming CEO he was very involved in design. In addition to Elon, whose impact on the company makes him a founder of sorts, the founding team was comprised of Martin Eberhard and Marc Tarpenning. Before founding Tesla, Martin and Marc had started a company together called NuvoMedia, which produced the Rocket eBook. The company was acquired by GemStar-TV Guide International for $187 million three years before Martin and Marc founded Tesla. It was actually not the financial ability but moral challenges with purchasing a gasoline-powered high-performance sports car that led Martin Eberhard to start investigating electric vehicles. More details are provided in Chapter 2.

Fisker was founded by Henrik Fisker, an automobile designer with a long history of designing beautiful luxury vehicles. Prior to focusing on building the Fisker Karma he had roles as CEO of BMW's Designworks/USA and was the chief designer at Aston Martin. Immediately before starting Fisker Karma, he founded Fisker Coachbuild, a company that purchased Mercedes SL and BMW M6 cars and did a process called "coach-building" (hence the name) in which the performance and design materials are upgraded. In Fisker Coachbuild's case, performance improvements were outsourced, while the company focused on things like changing out the LED lights and changing the leather used to a more natural untreated and soft leather. When the upgrades were complete Fisker Coachbuild sold these upgraded vehicles to a very affluent consumer for $199,000 to $369,500.[13]

Fisker Coachbuild was actually hired by Tesla for $800,000 to consult on the body and interior styling of the Tesla Model S sedan. At the time, Tesla didn't know Fisker was working on its own hybrid sedan. This consultation resulted in a lawsuit between the companies as Tesla felt Fisker had stolen secret proprietary information and incorporated it into the Karma.[14] Fisker won the lawsuit in arbitration, but bad blood remained between the companies. In an interview with *Automobile* magazine, Musk characterized the differences between them as follows:

> The fundamental problem with Henrik Fisker [is] he is a designer or stylist . . . he thinks the reason we don't have electric cars is for lack of styling. This is not the reason. It's fundamentally a technology problem. At the same time you need to make it look good and feel good, because otherwise you're going to have an impaired product. But just making something look like an electric car does not make it an electric car. [Fisker] thinks the most important thing in the world—or the only important thing in the world—is design, so he outsourced the engineering and manufacturing. But the fact is . . . that's the crux of the problem. And he's outsourcing to people who don't know how to solve the problem. So he came up with a product—it's a mediocre product at a high price. It looks good. Particularly from the side it looks good. I don't love the front. It looks too much like a caricature of a Mexican Bandito, the grille. The car looks very big, it's bigger than the Model S, but it has no trunk space and it's cramped inside, particularly in the rear seats. The mark of a good design is something that has great aesthetics and great functionality.[15]

Customer Traction

In the case of Fisker and Tesla, there are two key metrics on which we compared the companies' growth. First, we look at revenue growth. While it would take years for Tesla to achieve its first quarter of profitability, something it did not achieve until its first quarter of 2013,[16] unlike Tumblr and Posterous referenced above Tesla did charge customers for the product from the first day.

Tesla and Fisker Revenue (2008–2014)[17]

TABLE A.2

	Tesla	Fisker
2008	$14.7 M	
2009	$111.9 M	
2010	$116.7 M	
2011	$204.2 M	$28.1 M
2012	$413.3 M	$170.3 M
2013	$2 B	$8.6 M
2014	$3.2 B	

The other interesting metric to look at is just the total number of cars sold in the first few years of production. Tesla started delivering its first Roadster car in late 2008. Production was slow at first; in the first two months the company only produced five Roadster vehicles (March and April 2008)[18] but the company would go on to deliver over 100 vehicles by the end of 2008.[19] By May of 2009 Tesla had delivered another 400 for a total of 500 Roadsters.[20] Ultimately, the company would produce 2,600 Roadsters through the end of 2011 before shifting its focus to the Sedan (Model S).[21]

Fisker originally projected delivering the Karma in 2009, but didn't actually start delivering vehicles until 2011, when it delivered about 200 cars. The company's peak year of production was 2012 when it delivered 1,600 cars, before decreasing deliveries in 2013. In its few years of production, the company produced a total of 2,350 cars. As mentioned in the section on avoiding premature scaling, Fisker originally projected 15,000 Karmas a year, starting in late 2009.[22]

Exit

Tesla went public June 29, 2010, and closed its first day of trading at $23.89, or a market cap of $2.2 billion.[23] The company has continued to increase in value and as of October 21, 2015, was worth over $27 billion.[24] Fisker on the other hand ultimately declared bankruptcy and its assets were sold to Chinese auto-parts conglomerate Wanxiang Group.[25]

MINT VS WESABE

Product Overview

Mint and Wesabe were both web applications built to make it easier for individuals to manage their personal finances. While the products were very similar, as we described in more detail in the book, Mint was focused on simplicity and automatically categorized transactions even at the risk of sometimes categorizing them incorrectly. As Wesabe co-founder Marc Hedlund explained:

> Mint focused on making the user do almost no work at all, by automatically editing and categorizing their data, reducing the number of fields in their signup form, and giving them immediate gratification as soon as they possibly could; we completely sucked at all of that. Instead, I prioritized trying to build tools that would eventually help people change their financial behavior for the better, which I believed required people to more closely work with and understand their data. My goals may have been (okay, were) noble, but in the end we didn't help the people I wanted to since the product failed. I was focused on trying to make the usability of editing data as easy and functional as it could be; Mint was focused on making it so you never had to do that at all. Their approach completely kicked our approach's ass. (To be defensive for just a moment, their data accuracy—how well they automatically edited—was really low, and anyone who looked deeply into their data at Mint, especially in the beginning, was shocked at how inaccurate it was. The point, though, is hardly anyone seems to have looked.)[26]

Financing[27]

Figure A.3

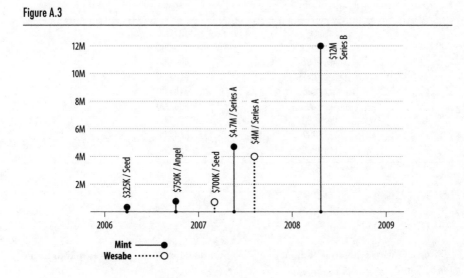

Leadership Team

Aaron Patzer founded Mint, where he served as the CEO through the company's sale to Intuit. Prior to founding Mint, he was an engineer with expertise in designing microprocessor, bioinformatics, and optical networking solutions. He has undergraduate and master's degrees in electrical engineering from Duke and Princeton, respectively.[28]

Wesabe was founded by Marc Hedlund and Jason Knight. While Jason was originally the CEO and co-founder, tragically his newborn son was diagnosed with a serious medical condition and he resigned, leaving Marc to transition from chief product officer to CEO.[29] Both Marc and Jason had impressive backgrounds before starting Wesabe. Marc was the founder and GM of the online unit for Lucas Films and was CEO at Popular Power.[30] Popular Power was a startup that focused on getting customers from across the Internet to download software that aggregated those computers' unused microprocessor cycles together to function in aggregate as a very powerful supercomputer.[31]

Customer Traction

The most important statistic for both Mint and Wesabe is the number of individuals using their web application. From the best data we were able to obtain, it appears that both services had about the same number of users in early 2008.[32] From January of 2008 to January of 2009, the number of unique visitors to Mint increased by a factor of 5.2x while Wesabe only increased by 0.6x. This traffic converted into customers; as table A.3 illustrates, Mint's growth took off considerably.

TABLE A.3

	Mint
February 2008[33]	135,000
April 2008[34]	180,000
Aug 2008	404,000
Sept 2008	458,000
Oct 2008	544,000
Nov 2008	606,000
Dec 2008	720,000
Jan 2009	864,000
Feb 2009	934,000

Exit

Ultimately, Wesabe ran out of money and was shut down in 2010. Mint was sold to Intuit for $170 million in 2009.

AUTOMATTIC (WORDPRESS) VS SIX APART (MOVABLE TYPE)

Product Overview

Automattic and Six Apart were both involved in the creation of blog platforms and provided commercial support around the communities interested in those platforms. Automattic's co-founder, Matt Mullenweg, was the founder of the WordPress open-source platform. The company continues to support the WordPress.com site and the VIP instances of Word-Press.com. Six Apart was best known for creating Movable Type, which it eventually open sourced,[35] and also the TypePad hosting platform. We talked in Chapter 6 about some of the missteps in their licensing communication.

It's worth pointing out that neither of these applications was the first to use tools that allowed individuals to write blog posts easily. Blogger, the first company to deliver that service at scale, came on the scene much earlier; it was ultimately sold to Google. As an interesting side note, Evan Williams—the founder of Blogger—and some of his early colleagues there would later go on to found Twitter.

What is interesting to me about both Movable Type (Six Apart) and WordPress (Automattic) is that these two companies created open-source software around this trend and then created for-profit businesses. While our focus is on the for-profit companies, it's impossible (and you really shouldn't try) to separate out the impact and scale of the software projects behind each company's founding.

Financing[36]

Figure A.4

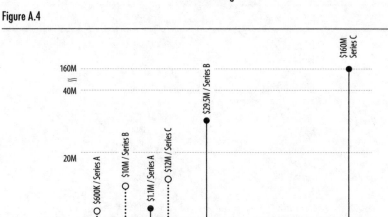

Leadership Team

Automattic was founded by Matt Mullenweg. The company name is a play on his name, Matt—hence the two "t"s in Automattic. Prior to founding Automattic, Matt started Word-Press as an open-source development project while a political science student at University of Houston. He dropped out of college to join CNET and help them with their blogging projects and then a year later (October 2005) moved full-time to focusing on WordPress and Automattic.[37]

The husband-and-wife team of Ben and Nina Trout founded Six Apart. The name was a reference to their being born six days apart. Nina and Ben had worked at a San Francisco web design consulting studio that shut down in 2001. When it shut down, they decided to work on their own blogging platform (Movable Type). While originally started as a side project, it grew much more rapidly than they expected and they eventually went on to raise venture capital.[38]

Customer Traction

Arguably the easiest comparison was to look at the traffic to Typepad.com (the hosted version of Movable Type) versus WordPress.com (the hosted version of WordPress). Word-Press.com traffic grew from roughly half the traffic of Typepad to equal over the second half of 2006.[39]

If you look at traffic from that point until today, the growth has been absolutely incredible. The chart below, based on information provided by the company, starts with traffic in October of 2006 and provides the number of page views across the WordPress.com network for the first month of every quarter through October 2011.[40]

TABLE A.4

Month	Number of Page Views
October 2006	25.5 Million
January 2007	126.6 Million
April 2007	186.5 Million
July 2007	377.1 Million
October 2007	531.4 Million
January 2008	775.2 Million
April 2008	1.064 Billion
July 2008	1.379 Billion
October 2008	1.827 Billion
January 2009	2.014 Billion
April 2009	2.293 Billion
July 2009	2.542 Billion
October 2009	2.880 Billion
January 2010	3.341 Billion
April 2010	3.629 Billion
July 2010	3.983 Billion
October 2010	4.804 Billion
January 2011	5.616 Billion
April 2011	6.161 Billion
July 2011	6.435 Billion
October 2011	7.407 Billion

Exit

While both companies are still privately held, the contrast in their outcome remains stark. Six Apart was ultimately merged with a video ad network startup, VideoEgg, to form SAY Media in an attempt to build a "new modern media company." At the time of the merger, SAY Media (and former VideoEgg) CEO Matt Sanchez said: "Movable Type and the TypePad platform will both be platforms that we'll keep around and continue to invest in."[41]

However, three months later SAY Media decided it needed to focus its resources and sold the Movable Type assets and the Six Apart brand to Infocomo, the Japanese IT services company.[42]

Automattic on the other hand continues to thrive, as does WordPress. Today more than one out of every five sites on the Internet is powered by WordPress[43] and the last financing round was rumored to value Automattic at over $1 billion.[44]

YOUTUBE VS REVVER

Product

YouTube and Revver were two of the early services focused on allowing consumers to upload, share, and watch streamed video online. The core product features were surprisingly similar. The biggest difference was Revver's early emphasis on sharing ad revenue with the individual who uploaded the video, while YouTube delayed validating and executing on a monetization strategy.

Financing[45]

Figure A.5—Financing Received by Revver and YouTube

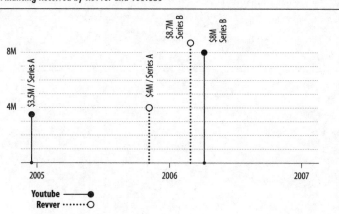

Leadership Team

YouTube was founded by three former PayPal employees: Chad Hurley, Steve Chen, and Jawed Karim. Jawed eventually left to pursue a graduate degree in computer science at Stanford. Chad and Steve remained at YouTube through the acquisition by Google.[46]

Revver was founded by Ian Clarke, Oliver Luckett, and Steven Starr. They were based in Los Angeles. Steven, the CEO, had experience working in the film industry both at Walt Disney and at the William Morris Agency. He also co-founded an early venture-backed startup called Upprizer, a peer-to-peer enterprise software company, on which Ian served as his CTO.[47]

Customer Traction

Both YouTube and Revver started showing significant growth drafting off MySpace in late 2006, but in January 2007 Revver was blocked by the social network because it was serving advertisements along with the videos, which was against the MySpace terms of use.[48]

Exit

YouTube was acquired by Google in 2006 for $1.65 billion.[49] While it is difficult to separate how much of the continuing increase in valuation is due to the support and resources of Google, analysts estimate YouTube would be worth between $26 billion and $40 billion as a stand-alone business today.[50] Revver on the other hand was sold to LiveUniverse for $5 million in 2008[51] and, as LiveUniverse struggled, was ultimately shut down.[52]

FACEBOOK VS FRIENDSTER
Product

Friendster and later Facebook were early iterations of social networks. While Facebook orig-inally restricted access to individuals attending certain colleges and then to college students in general, ultimately both networks had the same ambition: to create a web service to make it easier to track what your friends were doing.

Financing[53]

Figure A.6

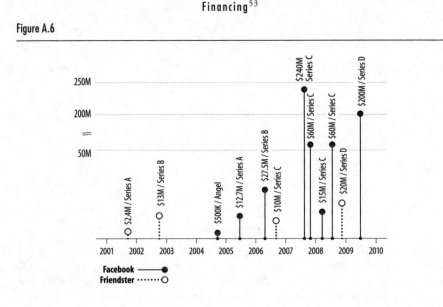

Leadership Team

While Mark Zuckerberg's control since the earliest days of Facebook is literally the stuff of Hollywood films, what is definitely clear is that Mark Zuckerberg—and only Mark Zuck-erberg—makes and always has made the strategic choices for Facebook.[54]

Friendster was founded by Jonathan Abrams, a Canadian engineer who moved to Sili-con Valley to join Netscape, where he worked for two years as an engineer. After leaving Netscape, he founded and was CEO of HotLinks. HotLinks was an early attempt to allow people to organize web pages based on their friends' bookmarks, a feature that would later be popularized by social book-marking sites. After that he launched Friendster, the first social network; in many ways he can be considered the inventor of the category. In fact, Friendster was later awarded the US patent for the concept of a social network.[55]

Customer Traction

Based on website traffic analysis done by comScore, in 2006 Facebook basically caught up to Friendster. However, over the next four years the networks' activity would separate—with

Facebook's traffic growing to over 600 million unique visitors while Friendster's traffic decreased.[56]

Exit

Ultimately Friendster was shut down and relaunched as a social platform, based in Malaysia, for games. Friendster also sold its patent portfolio of the concept of a social network (referenced above) to Facebook for a rumored $40 million purchase price.[57]

Facebook, on the other hand, scaled from being a network exclusively for college students to a social network with over one billion members and went public at a valuation of over $100 billion and is currently worth $273 billion.

LINKEDIN VS SPOKE
Product

LinkedIn and Spoke both aspired to build a professionally oriented social network. While they took different approaches and, like each pair of companies studied, ended up in different places, both started with the hypothesis that individuals wanted a different online presence for their work and personal profiles and networks.

Financing[58]

Figure A.7

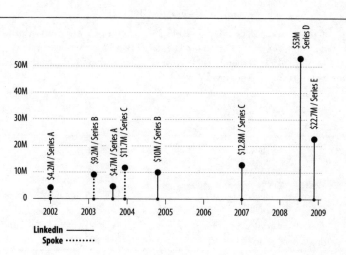

Leadership Team

The founding team of LinkedIn reads like an all-star team of Silicon Valley entrepreneurs, starting first and foremost with founding CEO Reid Hoffman. Reid was actually an investor in the Seed Round of Facebook and the Series A, B, and C rounds of Friendster. Earlier in his career he served on the board and as an executive VP at PayPal through its acquisition by eBay and before that he founded Socialnet.com, one of the earlier social networks online. He has an undergraduate degree from Stanford and a graduate degree from Oxford and started his career at Apple Computer, in user experience.[59]

Joining Reid at the start of the LinkedIn journey were four other exceptional entrepreneurs. Allen Blue was LinkedIn's VP of Product and had previously worked with Reid as director of product design at SocialNet.com and had also worked at PayPal and Microsoft. Konstantin Guericke was the VP of Marketing who had previously worked in marketing strategy and sales positioning in a variety of Silicon Valley startups and in contract roles, including VP of Marketing and Sales at another early social software company, Blaxxun.

LinkedIn's chief technology officer Eric Ly had already founded and sold an enterprise in project collaboration software to Critical Path (Nasdaq: CPTH). Finally, the only one of the founders not to have attended Stanford for at least part of his higher education, Jean-Luc Vaillant, was the VP of engineering. Like Allen, he had worked with Reid at SocialNet.com as director of technology and had a variety of other interesting work experiences, including doing early work in video at a company called Spotlife that was acquired by Logitech, for whom he continued as director of engineering for video services.[60]

Spoke was incubated inside the Silicon Valley Venture Capital firm US Venture Partners, in which CEO and co-founder Ben Smith was a partner.[61] Prior to starting Spoke, Ben was a senior advisor to the White House, helping create the TSA after the September 11 terrorist attack, and before that he was one of the youngest partners at the management-consulting firm AT Kearney.[62]

Customer Traction

LinkedIn officially launched on May 5, 2003. At the end of its first month in operation, LinkedIn had a total of 4,500 members in the network and grew slowly over the first year, finishing 2003 with 100,000 members.[63] However, the growth increased dramatically over the next few years as the chart below shows:

TABLE A.5

2004	2 million
2005	4 million
2006	8 million
2007	17 million
2008	32 million
2009	55 million
2010	90 million

Exit

While both sites are still operational today, the number of people impacted by their services and the financial value of the two entities couldn't be more different. Quantcast estimates Spoke receives less than 200,000 visitors a month while LinkedIn gets 75 million visitors from the United States every month. LinkedIn went on to go public in July 2011 and is currently valued at $25.7 billion.

HOTMAIL VS JUNO
Product

While you have to think back a decade, there was a time when everyone didn't have a personal email account that was untethered to their job or to the company providing them Internet access; and in many work environments email was not even a common communication channel. In fact, the idea for Hotmail—an email account you could access through any browser—came to the founders when they were collaborating on another idea and were unable to access their personal email accounts (a Stanford and AOL email account) from work. The entrepreneurs at Hotmail were the first to introduce a free (ultimately ad-supported) email account for everyone with access to a web browser.[64] While today Hotmail accounts are often seen as retro, at the time the service truly democratized personal email addresses to "normal" consumers.

Financing[65]

Figure A.8

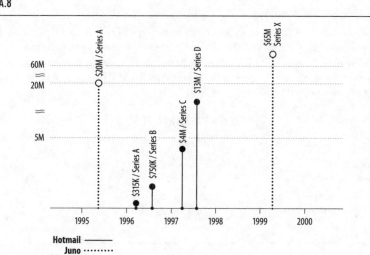

Leadership Team

Sabeer Bhatia and Jack Smith were the co-founders of Hotmail. The two met when they worked together at Apple and then continued to work together on a startup that ultimately wasn't successful before joining their talents to found Hotmail.

Jeff Bezos, who would later go on to start Amazon.com, was running a group inside the investment firm D. E. Shaw at the time, focused on looking at opportunities to leverage the firm's computer science expertise to expand it from investment management to creating Internet business.[66] One of the first companies created under this initiative was Juno, launched by Charles Ardai, then a 25-year-old Senior VP at D. E. Shaw.

Customer Traction

While both services monetized their free email network with advertisers, the most important metric for both businesses was the number of free email accounts being managed through the service. The chart below illustrates the early lead that Juno had over Hotmail at first, followed by Hotmail's rapid growth during 1997, and culminating in Hotmail's acquisition by Microsoft on New Year's Eve.[67]

TABLE A.6

	Juno	Hotmail
Launch Service	April 22, 1996	July 4, 1996
Late 1996	800,000 accounts (Dec)	100,000 (Sept)
July 1997	2.2 million accounts	4.5 million accounts
Acquisition by Microsoft (end of 1997)	3.5 million accounts	12 million accounts

Exit

On New Year's Eve 1997, Microsoft acquired Hotmail for $400 million. This concluded an amazing growth experience over 20 months. On the other hand, Juno went public in May 1999 and ultimately, after a flat IPO, went on to merge with NetZero about two years later, ending contentious litigation between the two companies.[68] That merged entity would ultimately roll into United Online.

CVENT VS STARCITE

Product

Cvent and StarCite both provide software to make it easier for corporations to manage in-person events.

Financing[69]

Figure A.9

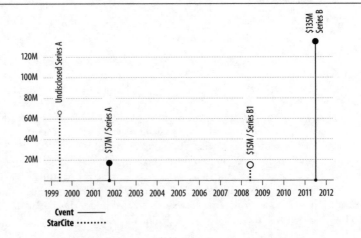

Leadership Team

Reggie Aggarwal is the founder and CEO of Cvent. Before starting Cvent, Reggie was a lawyer, receiving his JD from Washington and Lee and an LLM from Georgetown University. As a lawyer at the firm Shaw Pittman,[70] he founded the Indian CEO High Tech Council (now the DC Chapter of TiE). The experience of running events within this group led Reggie to create Cvent to automate the process.

Reggie was joined by four other co-founders: Chuck Ghoorah, who leads Sales and Marketing; David Quattrone, chief technology officer; Thomas Kramer, chief financial officer; and Dwayne Sye, chief information officer. In an amazing testament to the team's cohesiveness, 16 years after starting Cvent three of those four founders are still with the team.[71] The only exception is Thomas Kramer, who left to be the CFO of Opower.[72]

John Pino was the founder and CEO of StarCite through its merger with competitor OnVantage. Prior to launching StarCite, John was the president and CEO of McGettigan Partners, a $300 million meeting management company, giving him, like Reggie Aggarwal at Cvent, a good perspective on the process of planning and organizing meetings.[73]

Exit

Cvent went public in August 2013[74] and currently has a market cap of over $1.3 billion.

In late 2011, StarCite was acquired by Active Network for $51.8 million in a combination of cash and stock.[75]

MCDONALD'S VS WHITE CASTLE
Product

Founded in 1921 by Walter Anderson and E. W. Ingram, White Castle is considered to be the first hamburger chain. *The Oxford Encyclopedia of Food and Drink in America, Volume 1* notes, "The success of White Castle spawned countless imitators who closely copied White Castle's architecture, hamburgers, company names and even its advertising slogan." McDonald's did not arrive on the scene until 18 years later, when White Castle had over 100 locations established. It would take McDonald's until 1959 to match this number.[76]

Financing

One of the keys to McDonald's growth was the organization's ability to generate additional growth capital by leveraging franchising techniques and financing its real estate. On the other hand, White Castle refused to seek outside capital and avoided loans. We talked about this in detail in Chapter 11.

Leadership Team

McDonald's was founded by brothers Richard and Maurice McDonald in San Bernadino, California. However, the later addition of Ray Kroc as a third partner changed the trajectory of the business forever. Ray was a salesman who upon seeing McDonald's operations was immediately impressed and ultimately convinced the brothers to let him become a partner, later buying the brothers' stake. He started his career selling paper cups and, after rising up the sales organization, moved on and took a risk by joining Multimixer (a company manufacturing a milkshake blender), where he again rose up the sales organization. It was the eight Multimixers that McDonald's had purchased and used in parallel that led to Ray's interest in the hamburger chain.[77]

Walter Anderson and E. W. Ingram opened the first White Castle restaurant in Wichita, Kansas, in 1921. Anderson had some experience in the business: five years earlier he had opened another hamburger stand in the same location. In 1934, the company moved its headquarters to Columbus, Ohio, where it remains to this day.[78]

Customer Traction

As mentioned in the introduction to this pair of companies, above, by the time McDonald's arrived White Castle had over 100 locations in operation. Unfortunately, World War II would have an impact on White Castle due to rations on meat, reducing the number of restaurant units from 100 to 70. The company would not reach the 100-restaurant mark again until 1963.[79]

It was roughly during this time that McDonald's would truly take off. In 1959, McDonald's would exceed 100 locations, opening 67 restaurants that year. Over the next ten years that number would increase by more than a factor of ten, with McDonald's opening store number 1,000 in 1968. The growth continued and today McDonald's operates over 31,000 restaurants.

Exit

White Castle remains a privately held company to this day, with less than 500 locations.

McDonald's is a publicly traded corporation and today has a market capitalization of over $90 billion. In the foreword of *McDonald's: Behind the Arches,* a book on McDonald's business success, author John Love puts the company's incredible growth into context:

> In an industry that has nearly 200,000 separate restaurant companies, how many would even guess that McDonald's captures 14 percent of all restaurant visits in the United States—one out of every six—and commands 6.6 percent share of all dollars Americans spend on eating out? How many would know that it controls 18.3 percent of the $72 billion fast-food market in the United States—more than the next three chains combined? How many would suspect that McDonald's sells 34 percent of all hamburgers sold by commercial restaurants and 26 percent of all french fries.[80]

GOOGLE
Product

Google created a search engine whose algorithms are able to return incredibly accurate search results; its revenue is primarily derived from the sale of ads. While originally just a search engine, Google has now expanded its competencies to cover a wide array of Internet-related services.

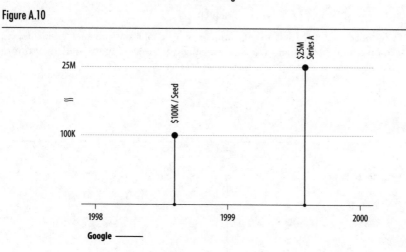

Financing[81]

Figure A.10

Leadership Team[82]

Google was started by co-founders Larry Page and Sergey Brin who met at Stanford University where they were both pursuing PhDs in computer science. Together they started a side project and developed the idea of a search engine company. In 1998, with this side project taking up more and more of their time, Larry and Sergey decided to drop out of the PhD program and launch Google from a friend's garage in Menlo Park, California. Eric Schmidt was brought on as CEO after Google's second funding round.

Customer Traction

When Google was founded in September 1998, it was serving ten thousand search queries per day. One year after being launched, Google was already answering 3.5 million search queries daily. In mid-2000 Google was handling 18 million queries per day on average.[83] By the time Google announced its IPO in April 2004, users around the world were submitting more than 200 million queries to Google every day. Today Google handles about 3.5 billion searches per day.[84]

Exit

On August 19, 2004, Google went public in a highly anticipated initial public offering that valued the young company at $23 billion. Today Google has a market cap of $440.2 billion.[85]

PAYPAL

Product

Formally founded in 2001, PayPal is an online payment solutions provider. It enables its users to transact money through their account balances, bank accounts, and credit cards, without having to share financial information with other users.

Financing[86]

Figure A.11

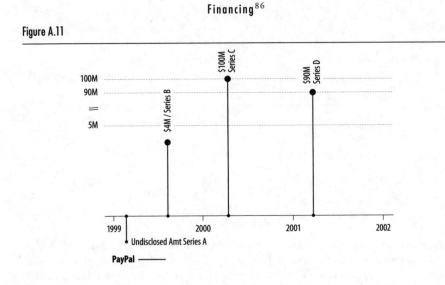

Leadership Team

PayPal is the result of two companies merging together. Peter Thiel and Max Levchin founded a company called Confinity. The main focus of the company was PalmPilot cryptography, and more specifically, money transfers between PalmPilot owners. The other half of what eventually became PayPal was X.com. The main focus of X.com was general financial services, including payments by email. X.com was founded and run by Elon Musk. The two companies merged with the idea that they would focus on Internet-based payment services.

Customer Traction[87]

TABLE A.7

October 1999	Launch
March 2000	1,200 accounts
December 31, 2000	4 million accounts
June 30, 2001	8.8 million accounts

Exit

Technically, there were two exits for PayPal; Exit 1 was an IPO in 2002 and Exit 2 occurred shortly after PayPal's IPO, when the company was acquired by eBay in July 2002 for $1.5 billion.

DROPBOX
Product

Dropbox, founded in 2007, is a file-sharing service that allows users to save photos, videos, docs, and other files. Any file you save to your Dropbox is automatically saved to all your computers, phones or tablets, and the Dropbox website, making it incredibly easy for you to access and share your files.

Financing[88]

Figure A.12

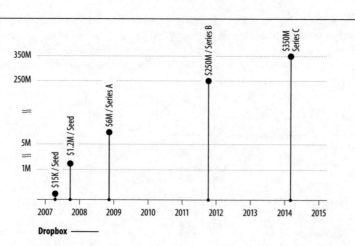

Leadership Team

Dropbox was founded by Drew Houston, an MIT computer science student, who had the idea for a better file-sharing service after forgetting his thumb drive on a bus trip from Boston to NYC. He applied to Y Combinator as a solo founder but was eventually joined by fellow MIT student Arash Ferdowsi, whom Houston had met in Silicon Valley.[89]

Customer Traction

Dropbox grew quickly as a company despite spending very little on advertising. With almost no prior marketing experience, the Dropbox team created a simple video that they posted on Digg in March 2008—this video helped them go from 5,000 people on the wait list to a 75,000-person wait list. The Dropbox team then slowly let people in off of this wait list. Dropbox went live in early 2009 and tried to do traditional paid advertising through Google AdWords, a tactic that failed miserably. However, the company was still doing pretty well, having reached one million users just seven months after launch. Then in early 2010 Dropbox instituted a referral program inspired by a similar program used by PayPal. Through this referral program Dropbox went from 100,000 users to over four million in just 14 months after launch, meaning Dropbox had an impressive 28 percent growth rate. Unlike PayPal, Dropbox gave away extra storage for each new referral. Today Dropbox has over 400 million users.[90]

Exit

The last round of financing was $500 million of debt financing, on April 6, 2014. There are continued rumors that Dropbox is headed to an IPO at some point soon.

AIRBNB

Product

Airbnb is a website that provides a marketplace for people to rent out lodging in their spare rooms or home. Users of the site must register and create a personal online profile before using the site. Every property is associated with a host whose profile includes recommendations by other users, reviews by previous guests, as well as a response rating.

Financing[91]

Figure A.13

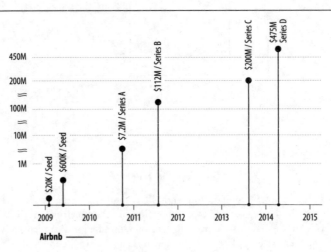

Leadership Team

Airbnb was founded in San Francisco, California, by Nathan Blecharczyk, Brian Chesky, and Joe Gebbia in August 2008. Brian and Joe came up with the idea after struggling to pay rent and realizing they could make money by renting space in their house. They set up a website and hosted their first three guests who were in town for a conference. They invited Nathan, a former roommate, to help them build the company.[92]

Customer Traction

While initial growth was slow, Airbnb was eventually able to achieve high growth through its use of better photography and using large conferences like the Democratic National Convention as a springboard to grow its user base. After growing by just one million guests served between 2008 and 2011, Airbnb took off in 2012, adding three million guests served. This growth has continued: Over ten million guests have now stayed at a place listed on Airbnb.[93]

Exit

The last round of financing for Airbnb was $1.5 billion in private equity on June 28, 2015.

UBER

Product

Uber is a technology company that developed the Uber app, which allows consumers with smartphones to submit trip requests which are then routed to the smartphones of Uber drivers, who use their own cars to pick up riders.

Financing

Figure A.14

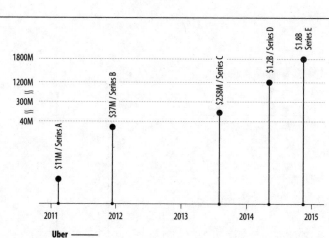

Leadership Team

Uber was founded in 2009 by Travis Kalanick and Garrett Camp. Both Garrett and Travis had successfully founded startups prior to Uber. Garrett Camp founded StumbleUpon, a popular web-discovery platform, while Travis founded Red Swoosh, a peer-to-peer file-sharing system. This prior experience in successful startups allowed the two to develop Uber quickly and efficiently while also leveraging their connections to secure financing.[94]

Customer Traction

Uber has taken a city-by-city strategy in the release of its product. Starting in San Francisco, Uber was able to get between 3,000 and 6,000 users and had done between 10,000 and 20,000 rides in just the first six months of operation. This gave it a growth rate of approximately 35 percent, which has only recently begun to slow down as Uber has fewer options for expanding into new cities.[95]

While adding users, Uber also had to add drivers. It has increased its active driver base from basically zero in mid-2012 to over 160,000 at the end of 2014. Over 55 percent of the US population now has access to Uber.[96]

Exit

While still a privately held company, Uber's latest financing round was a Series E round of $1 billion on February 18, 2015.

TWITTER
Product

Twitter is an online social networking site that allows registered users to send and read short 140-character messages called "tweets." Twitter was created in March 2006 as a spin-off of the company Odeo.

Financing[97]

Figure A.15

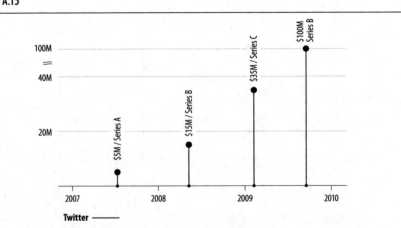

Twitter ———

Leadership Team

The credited founders for Twitter are Jack Dorsey, Evan Williams, Biz Stone, and Noah Glass. While Noah Glass exited the company early on, the others have continued to play a role in Twitter's successful growth. Evan Williams was the most experienced of the Twitter founders; he had previously founded Blogger and is credited with having invented the term "blog." He brought this prior experience and success to a company called Odeo where he teamed up with Jack Dorsey, Biz Stone, and Noah Glass to create a product that would eventually become Twitter.

Customer Traction

While Twitter had good initial growth, what launched its growth to transform it into the company we know today was its 2007 visit to the tech and music festival SxSW in Austin, Texas. After SxSW, Twitter grew by an astounding 752 percent, for a total of 4.43 million unique visitors in December 2008, after starting the year with only around 500,000 unique monthly visitors. Its use of the SxSW event as a springboard allowed Twitter to gain real traction among users. Twitter now has more than 500 million users.[98]

Exit

Twitter filed an IPO and opened trading on November 7, 2013, and now has a market cap of $20.66 billion.

NOTES

CHAPTER 1

1. "College Startups on the Rise as Students Flock to Entrepreneurial Pursuits," *Red Herring*, August 15, 2014, http://www.redherring.com/startups/college-startups-on-the-rise-as-students-flock-to-entrepreneurial-pursuits/
2. Melissa Korn, "B-Schools Vie for Startup Crown," *Wall Street Journal*, December 4, 2013, http://www.wsj.com/news/articles/SB10001424052702303722104579238153471481082?KEYWORDS=melissa+korn&mg=reno64-wsj
3. https://www.youtube.com/watch?v=OgO4I3_B0Js
4. Value as of 10/21/2015
5. http://techcrunch.com/2014/02/24/dropbox-filing/
6. http://www.wsj.com/articles/the-secret-math-of-airbnbs-24-billion-valuation-1434568517
7. http://www.wsj.com/articles/uber-valued-at-more-than-50-billion-1438367457
8. http://www.cnet.com/news/yahoo-dumps-google-search-technology/
9. http://blog.precipice.org/why-wesabe-lost-to-mint/
10. We did not include Tesla and Fisker in this table, because the Series A & B financing amounts were not disclosed for Fisker Automotive.
11. "The Importance of Young Firms for Economic Growth," *Entrepreneurship Policy Digest*, September 25, 2014, http://www.kauffman.org/~/media/kauffman_org/resources/2014/entrepreneurship%20policy%20digest/september%202014/entrepreneurship_policy_digest_september2014.pdf
12. http://techcrunch.com/2015/03/17/these-are-the-top-20-us-accelerators/

SECTION I

1. http://blog.startupcompass.co/pages/startup-genome-report-extra-on-premature-scal

CHAPTER 2

1. James Burley and Greg A. Stevens, "Piloting the Rocket of Radical Innovation," *Research Technology Management*, 2003, p. 16.
2. http://www.businessinsider.com/tesla-the-origin-story-2014-10

3. http://www.nytimes.com/1994/01/28/business/expecting-a-fizzle-gm-puts-electric
    -car-to-test.html?pagewanted=all
4. http://www.washingtonpost.com/wp-dyn/articles/A21991-2005Mar9.html
5. http://www.washingtonpost.com/wp-dyn/articles/A21991-2005Mar9.html
6. March 13, 2007, Issue of *Newsweek* "Comin' Through!" GM R&D chief Larry Burns.
    https://en.wikipedia.org/wiki/General-Motors_EV1
7. http://www.businessinsider.com/tesla-the-origin-story-2014-10
8. http://www.businessinsider.com/tesla-the-origin-story-2014-10
9. http://www.automobilemag.com/features/news/1208_q_and_a_elon_musk_ceo
    _tesla/
10. http://www.automobilemag.com/features/news/1208_q_and_a_elon_musk_ceo
    _tesla/involvement.html
11. https://www.youtube.com/watch?v=L-s_3b5fRd8 Foundation 20 // Elon Musk
    (starting at minute 12)
12. http://reidhoffman.org/information-age-networked-age-network-literate/
13. http://mixergy.com/interviews/konstantin-guericke-linkedin-interview/
14. http://reidhoffman.org/linkedin-pitch-to-greylock/
15. http://bits.blogs.nytimes.com/2008/11/06/zuckerbergs-law-of-information
    -sharing/?_r=0&pagewanted=all
16. http://techcrunch.com/2011/07/06/mark-zuckerberg-explains-his-law-of-social
    -sharing-video/
17. Noah Kagan, *How I Lost 170 Million Dollars: My Time as #30 at Facebook* (Lioncrest
    Publishing, 2014), Kindle Edition, p. 25.
18. http://www.bloomberg.com/bw/magazine/content/11_21/b4229050473695.htm
19. Ray Kroc, *Grinding It Out: The Making of McDonald's* (Chicago: Contemporary
    Books, 1977), p 81.
20. Kroc, *Grinding It Out,* p. 83.
21. http://news.cnet.com/Yahoo-acquires-Oddpost-to-bolster-e-mail/2100-1038_3-52
    66019.html
22. http://toni.org/2014/01/13/a-new-ceo-for-automattic/
23. http://on.aol.com/video/jack-dorsey—co-founder-of-twitter-and-square—delivers
    -his-keynote-517474731
24. John P. Kotter and James L. Heskett, *Corporate Culture and Performance* (New York:
    The Free Press, 1992).
25. http://www.mensjournal.com/magazine/elon-musk-s-risky-business-20120803
26. Kroc, *Grinding It Out,* p 15.
27. John F. Love, *McDonald's: Behind the Arches* (New York: Bantam Books, 1995), pp.
    34–38.
28. Love, *McDonald's,* pp. 175–76.
29. http://techcrunch.com/2011/07/20/there-and-back-again-how-cvents-founder
    -stood-by-his-company-for-better-or-bankruptcy/

CHAPTER 3

1. http://pmarchive.com/guide_to_startups_part4.html
2. John Love, *McDonald's: Behind the Arches* (New York: Bantam Books, 1995), pp.
    122–26.
3. http://www.theglobeandmail.com/report-on-business/rob-magazine/invest-like
    -a-legend-timothy-draper/article22637614/

4. https://twitter.com/levie/status/475787246885277696
5. http://www.dtic.upf.edu/~alozano/innovation/
6. http://abovethecrowd.com/2014/07/11/how-to-miss-by-a-mile-an-alternative-look
    -at-ubers-potential-market-size/
7. http://blogs.wsj.com/digits/2014/06/06/uber-ceo-travis-kalanick-were-doubling
    -revenue-every-six-months/
8. http://mixergy.com/interviews/konstantin-guericke-linkedin-interview/
9. http://www.nytimes.com/2006/07/19/business/19electric.html?module=Search&
    mabReward=relbias%3Ar%2C%7B%221%22%3A%22RI%3A6%22%7D&
    _r=1&&pagewanted=all
10. http://www.dailydot.com/business/origin-tumblr-anarchaia-projectionist-david
    -karp/
11. http://avc.com/2010/11/self-expression-matters/
12. http://techcrunch.com/2010/11/12/tumblr-1540-percent-pageview-growth/
13. www.wired.co.uk/magazine/archive/2012/03/features/tumbling-on-success

CHAPTER 4

1. http://www.paulgraham.com/startupmistakes.html
2. Peter Thiel and Blake Masters, *Zero to One: Notes on Startups, or How to Build the
    Future* (New York: Crown Business, 2014), p. 48.
3. Ibid., p. 49.
4. https://www.youtube.com/watch?v=_sajNwt8ldI
5. https://www.youtube.com/watch?v=IQNmph8vObY
6. http://www.startuplessonslearned.com/2009/08/minimum-viable-product-guide
    .html
7. http://www.netpromoter.com/why-net-promoter/know
8. http://www.startup-marketing.com/using-survey-io/

CHAPTER 5

1. G. K. Chesterton, *On Lying in Bed and Other Essays* (Bayeux Arts, 2004), Kindle Edi-
    tion, locations 1873–1874.
2. http://edition.cnn.com/2014/02/13/tech/web/youtube-unboxing-videos/
3. http://mobile.nytimes.com/2014/08/17/magazine/a-mothers-journey-through-the
    -unnerving-universe-of-unboxing-videos.html?_r=2&referrer=&pagewanted=all
4. http://www.latimes.com/entertainment/tv/la-et-hgtv-cable-network-20th-anniver
    sary-20140720-story.html#page=2
5. http://www.shirky.com/writings/group_enemy.html
6. http://media.looops.net/saito/2012/01/16/20_hot_startup/
7. http://www.cnet.com/news/remember-friendster-thought-so/
8. Noah Kagan, *How I Lost 170 Million Dollars: My Time as #30 at Facebook* (Lioncrest
    Publishing, 2014), Kindle Edition, pp. 51–52.
9. http://www.informationweek.com/desktop/web-20-summit-twitter-founder-evan
    -williams-preaches-added-constraints/d/d-id/1060543
10. http://web.archive.org/web/19981212034238/http://www.yahoo.com/
11. http://web.archive.org/web/19981202230410/http://www.google.com/
12. Ray Kroc, *Grinding It Out: The Making of McDonald's* (Chicago: Contemporary
    Books, 1977), p. 9.

13. Ibid., p. 84.
14. http://www.mcdonalds.com/us/en/our_story/our_history/the_ray_kroc_story.html
15. http://www.majordojo.com/2011/02/how-did-wordpress-win.php
16. http://blog.precipice.org/why-wesabe-lost-to-mint/
17. http://www.nytimes.com/2006/10/15/business/yourmoney/15friend.html?_r=1&&pagewanted=all
18. http://www.nytimes.com/2006/10/15/business/yourmoney/15friend.html?_r=1&&pagewanted=all
19. http://mashable.com/2014/02/03/jonathan-abrams-friendster-facebook/
20. http://www.nytimes.com/2006/10/15/business/yourmoney/15friend.html?_r=1&&pagewanted=all
21. http://www.nngroup.com/articles/why-you-only-need-to-test-with-5-users/
22. http://techcrunch.com/2009/10/05/twitter-data-analysis-an-investors-perspective-2/. Emphasis added.
23. https://medium.com/user-experience-design-1/examining-first-time-use-4aea16bf7b3a

SECTION II

1. https://www.acs.org/content/acs/en/careers/whatchemistsdo/careers/catalytic-chemistry.html

CHAPTER 6

1. https://www.prezly.com/public-relations-quotes
2. http://www.startuplessonslearned.com/2009/03/dont-launch.html
3. http://qr.ae/t1oFi
4. http://arstechnica.com/uncategorized/2008/11/did-lazy-sunday-make-youtubes-1-5-billion-sale-possible/
5. http://money.cnn.com/2012/09/06/technology/airbnb-dnc-startup/
6. http://mixergy.com/interviews/konstantin-guericke-linkedin-interview/
7. http://www.forbes.com/sites/jjcolao/2012/09/05/the-internets-mother-tongue/
8. http://www.majordojo.com/2011/02/how-did-wordpress-win.php
9. http://www.aripaparo.com/archive/001008.html
10. http://nowaitapp.com/augusta
11. https://web.archive.org/web/20040605224615/http://www.sixapart.com/corner/archives/2004/05/its_about_time.shtml
12. https://web.archive.org/web/20040605224615/http://www.sixapart.com/corner/archives/2004/05/its_about_time.shtml
13. https://wordpress.org/news/2004/05/new-pricing-scheme/
14. https://wordpress.org/news/2004/05/moving-guide/
15. http://carthik.net/blog/vault/2004/05/14/movabletype-to-wordpress/

CHAPTER 7

1. https://twitter.com/paulg/status/533044876925865984
2. http://blakemasters.com/post/22405055017/peter-thiels-cs183-startup-class-9-notes-essay
3. http://www.fastcompany.com/1837839/reid-hoffman-paypals-pivoted-path-success

4. http://ecorner.stanford.edu/authorMaterialInfo.html?mid=1031
5. http://www.fastcompany.com/1837839/reid-hoffman-paypals-pivoted-path-success
6. http://techcrunch.com/2006/10/16/myspace-makes-subtle-shifts-to-emphasize
    -video/
7. http://youtube-global.blogspot.com/search?updated-min=2005-01-01T00:00:00
    -08:00&updated-max=2006-01-01T00:00:00-08:00&max-results=15
8. https://gigaom.com/2010/03/19/how-much-did-it-cost-to-start-youtube/
9. http://www.techrepublic.com/article/how-the-paypal-mafia-redefined-success-in
    -silicon-valley/
10. http://mashable.com/2006/08/01/youtube-now-more-popular-than-myspace/
11. http://www.prnewswire.com/news-releases/interactive-live-video-community—
    next-generation-social-network-livevideocom-joins-forces-with-top-online-content
    -creator-hub-revver-56802212.html
12. http://avc.com/2007/09/biz-stone-on-re/
13. http://mashable.com/2012/08/16/twitter-api-big-changes/
14. Note: The campaign that AirBnB undertook is said to have used "black hat" or tech-
    nically illegal tactics such as spamming craigslist posters.
15. https://growthhackers.com/companies/airbnb/
16. http://www.inc.com/magazine/201109/inc-500-brian-halligan-hubspot.html
17. http://labs.openviewpartners.com/how-to-build-a-channel-sales-program/
18. http://www.inc.com/cameron-albert-deitch/seven-takeaways-marc-andreessen-peter
    -thiel.html

CHAPTER 8

1. http://www.wsj.com/articles/SB10001424053111903480904576512250915629460
2. http://www.pewinternet.org/fact-sheets/mobile-technology-fact-sheet/
3. http://www.netflixprize.com/assets/NetflixPrizeKDD_to_appear.pdf
4. http://www.nytimes.com/2009/09/22/technology/internet/22netflix.html?_r=0
    &pagewanted=all
5. http://techblog.netflix.com/2012/04/netflix-recommendations-beyond-5-stars.html
6. https://chitika.com/google-positioning-value
7. http://hbswk.hbs.edu/item/6833.html
8. http://www.google.com/trends/explore#q=personal%20finance%20software%2C
    %20money%20help&cmpt=q&tz=
9. http://contently.com/strategist/2015/03/23/how-mint-turned-content-into-a-big
    -business/
10. https://blog.kissmetrics.com/how-mint-grew/
11. http://www.reddit.com/about/
12. https://www.crunchbase.com/person/stew-langille
13. http://contently.com/strategist/2015/03/23/how-mint-turned-content-into-a-big
    -business/
14. https://blog.kissmetrics.com/how-mint-grew/
15. http://readwrite.com/2010/05/03/mint_comes_to_android
16. http://readwrite.com/2011/03/12/sxsw-mint-talks-mobile-app-development-chal
    lenges-teases-new-ipad-app
17. http://www.inc.com/kelsey-libert/how-airbnb-is-spearheading-emotional-content
    -interview.html

18. http://www.inc.com/kelsey-libert/how-airbnb-is-spearheading-emotional-content
    -interview.html
19. http://www.inc.com/kelsey-libert/how-airbnb-is-spearheading-emotional-content
    -interview.html
20. https://ourstory.linkedin.com/#year-2006
21. http://www.consumeraffairs.com/online/spoke.html
22. http://blog.spoke.com/2012/02/spoke-privacy-is-major-concern-of-mine.html
23. http://www.nytimes.com/2014/11/17/business/media/airbnb-introducing-print
    -magazine-pineapple.html?pagewanted=all
24. http://www.campaignlive.com/article/airbnb-runs-berlin-wall-anniversary-camp
    aign/1321016#9tw6t2FpEvhCCYhp.99

CHAPTER 9

1. http://www.forentrepreneurs.com/lessons-learnt-viral-marketing/
2. http://dfj.com/news/article_25.shtml
3. http://dfj.com/news/article_25.shtml
4. Peter Thiel and Blake Masters, *Zero to One: Notes on Startups, or How to Build the Future* (New York: Crown Business, 2014), Kindle Edition, p. 137.
5. http://www.slideshare.net/gueste94e4c/dropbox-startup-lessons-learned-3836587
6. One interesting side note: Ben Parr would go on to be a very influential tech journalist as the Editor-at-Large for *Mashable*, one of the early technology blogs focused on social media, and later founded a seed stage fund called "Dominate Fund" with the support of a number of Hollywood celebrities. So you never know who your critics are, or who they may become!
7. http://content.time.com/time/nation/article/0,8599,1532225,00.html
8. http://www.merriam-webster.com/dictionary/gamification
9. http://www.gartner.com/newsroom/id/1629214

CHAPTER 10

1. http://www.mckinsey.com/insights/business_technology/big_data_the_next_fron
    tier_for_innovation
2. http://www.computerweekly.com/feature/What-does-a-petabyte-look-like
3. http://business.financialpost.com/entrepreneur/a-footnote-to-history-is-still-shoot
    ing-for-the-moon
4. http://www.businessmanagementdaily.com/43635/he-made-history-with-a-two
    -liter-bottle
5. http://radar.oreilly.com/2011/09/building-data-science-teams.html
6. https://hbr.org/2012/10/data-scientist-the-sexiest-job-of-the-21st-century/
7. http://radar.oreilly.com/2011/09/building-data-science-teams.html
8. https://hbr.org/2012/10/data-scientist-the-sexiest-job-of-the-21st-century/
9. http://radar.oreilly.com/2011/09/building-data-science-teams.html
10. https://hbr.org/2012/10/data-scientist-the-sexiest-job-of-the-21st-century/
11. https://fbcdn-dragon-a.akamaihd.net/hphotos-ak-prn1/851575_520797877991079
    _393255490_n.pdf
12. https://www.youtube.com/watch?v=bKZiXAFeBeY
13. https://medium.com/@gem_ray/a-year-of-designing-at-facebook-74ba9c292888
14. https://www.udemy.com/lean-startup-sxsw-2012-videos-and-presentations/#
    /lecture/76819

15. http://mixergy.com/interviews/konstantin-guericke-linkedin-interview/
16. http://mixergy.com/interviews/konstantin-guericke-linkedin-interview/
17. http://nerds.airbnb.com/experiments-at-airbnb/
18. https://www.youtube.com/watch?v=bKZiXAFeBeY
19. http://automattic.com/work-with-us/
20. Scott Berkun, *The Year without Pants: WordPress.com and the Future of Work* (San Francisco: Josey Bass Books, 2013), Kindle Edition, p. 60.
21. Ibid.
22. Jonathan Rosenberg and Eric Schmidt, *How Google Works* (New York: Grand Central Publishing, 2014), Kindle Edition.
23. http://nerds.airbnb.com/experiments-at-airbnb/
24. http://nerds.airbnb.com/experiments-at-airbnb/
25. http://www.nature.com/nrd/journal/v10/n9/full/nrd3545.html
26. http://online.wsj.com/news/articles/SB10001424052970203764804577059841672541590
27. http://www.plosmedicine.org/article/info:doi/10.1371/journal.pmed.0020124
28. http://www.kaushik.net/avinash/difference-web-reporting-web-analysis/
29. Ibid.
30. http://www.carscoops.com/2008/01/detroit-show-2009-fisker-karma-details.html
31. https://gigaom.com/2013/12/09/in-case-you-still-care-fiskers-three-years-of-sales-revealed/
32. http://www.statista.com/statistics/287753/large-luxury-vehicles-sales-by-make-in-the-united-states/
33. https://gigaom.com/2013/04/17/a-look-under-the-hood-why-electric-car-start up-fisker-crashed-and-burned/
34. https://www.udemy.com/lean-startup-sxsw-2012-videos-and-presentations/#/lecture/76819
35. http://business.financialpost.com/entrepreneur/a-footnote-to-history-is-still-shoot ing-for-the-moon

CHAPTER 11

1. https://www.twilio.com/customers/stories/uber
2. https://www.kickstarter.com/hello
3. John F. Love, *McDonald's: Behind the Arches* (New York: Bantam Books, 1995), p. 162.
4. http://gigaom.com/cleantech/ray-lane-kleiner-is-not-moving-away-from-greentech/
5. http://techcrunch.com/2011/07/20/there-and-back-again-how-cvents-founder -stood-by-his-company-for-better-or-bankruptcy/
6. https://www.youtube.com/watch?v=YK4mZQkfBZ8 @ 13:50 into interview
7. http://fortune.com/2015/06/18/marc-andreessen-talks-about-that-time-facebook -almost-lost-80-of-its-value/
8. https://medium.com/@bchesky/7-rejections-7d894cbaa084
9. https://www.crunchbase.com/organization/airbnb
10. http://fortune.com/2011/05/26/how-linkedin-first-raised-money-and-endured -rejection/

CHAPTER 12

1. Reid Hoffman and Ben Casnocha, *The Startup of You* (New York: Crown Business, 2012).

2. https://hbr.org/2014/04/the-ceo-of-automattic-on-holding-auditions-to-build-a -strong-team

3. Scott Berkun, *The Year without Pants: WordPress.com and the Future of Work* (San Francisco: Jossey Bass, 2013), Kindle Edition, p. 24.

4. http://davemart.in/2015/04/22/inside-automattics-remote-hiring-process/

5. https://hbr.org/2014/04/the-ceo-of-automattic-on-holding-auditions-to-build-a -strong-team

6. Laszlo Bock, *Work Rules!: Insights from Inside Google That Will Transform How You Live and Lead* (New York: Grand Central Publishing, 2015), Kindle Edition, p. 69.

7. Eric Schmidt and Jonathan Rosenberg, *How Google Works* (New York: Grand Central Publishing, 2014), Kindle Edition.

8. http://ma.tt/2011/09/automattic-creed/

9. Scott Berkun, *The Year without Pants*, p. 24.

10. http://aviariana.hamsaperet.com/building_trust_-_welcoming_employees.pdf

11. http://www.businessinsider.com/interview-with-nuzzel-ceo-jonathan-abrams-2015 -6#ixzz3dWRRMdj8

12. http://techcrunch.com/2011/07/20/there-and-back-again-how-cvents-founder-stood -by-his-company-for-better-or-bankruptcy/

13. http://www.smartceo.com/cvent-poised-take-reins-500-billion-meetings-events-in dustry/

14. Bock, *Work Rules!*, p. 77.

15. http://davemart.in/2015/04/22/inside-automattics-remote-hiring-process/

16. https://hbr.org/2014/04/the-ceo-of-automattic-on-holding-auditions-to-build-a -strong-team

17. http://techcrunch.com/2011/07/20/there-and-back-again-how-cvents-founder -stood-by-his-company-for-better-or-bankruptcy/

18. Bock, *Work Rules!*, p. 112.

19. http://www.gallup.com/poll/181289/majority-employees-not-engaged-despite -gains-2014.aspx

20. Jennifer A. Chatman, David F. Caldwell, Charles A. O'Reilly, and Bernadette Doerr, "Parsing Organizational Culture: How the Norm for Adaptability Influences the Relationship between Culture Consensus and Financial Performance in High-Technology," http://onlinelibrary.wiley.com/doi/10.1002/job.1928/abstract

21. Ibid.

22. Bock, *Work Rules!*, p. 70.

23. Ibid., p. 69.

24. Schmidt and Rosenberg, *How Google Works*.

25. http://www.washingtonpost.com/blogs/innovations/wp/2013/06/21/why-google -interviews-will-still-be-hard/

CHAPTER 13

1. Noah Kagan, *How I Lost 170 Million Dollars: My Time as #30 at Facebook* (Lioncrest Publishing, 2014), Kindle Edition, pp. 65–66.

2. http://www.nytimes.com/2006/10/15/business/yourmoney/15friend.html?_r=1

3. http://mavenventures.tumblr.com/post/23238841136/10-key-lessons-facebook -learned-from-friendster

4. http://www.automobilemag.com/features/news/1208_q_and_a_elon_musk_ceo _tesla/

5. Ibid.
6. http://www.businessinsider.com/tesla-the-origin-story-2014-10
7. Ibid.
8. http://www.quora.com/What-happened-to-Revver
9. http://news.bbc.co.uk/2/hi/business/6305957.stm
10. https://www.techdirt.com/articles/20060217/1016214.shtml
11. http://www.amazon.com/Habits-Highly-Effective-People-Powerful/dp/1451639619/
12. http://www.businessinsider.com/dwight-eisenhower-nailed-a-major-insight-about-productivity-2014-4
13. http://blog.idonethis.com/manager-focus-peter-thiel-paypal/
14. Ibid.
15. http://nerds.airbnb.com/the-antidote-to-bureaucracy-is-good-judgement/
16. http://www.joelonsoftware.com/articles/TwoStories.html
17. https://www.scrumalliance.org/why-scrum
18. https://www.youtube.com/watch?v=2Jhf7PcYrzY

CHAPTER 14

1. Eric Schmidt and Jonathan Rosenberg, *How Google Works* (New York: Grand Central Publishing, 2014), Kindle Edition.
2. http://www.wired.com/2012/05/network-effects-and-global-domination-the-facebook-strategy/all/1
3. http://blog.simeonov.com/2006/07/26/metcalfes-law-more-misunderstood-than-wrong/
4. http://www.wired.co.uk/magazine/archive/2012/03/features/tumbling-on-success
5. http://abovethecrowd.com/2012/11/13/all-markets-are-not-created-equal-10-factors-to-consider-when-evaluating-digital-marketplaces/
6. http://www.cvent.com/en/company/rfp-management-system.shtml
7. Cvent 2014 Annual Report: http://investors.cvent.com/~/media/Files/C/Cvent-IR/documents/annual-report-2014.pdf
8. http://www.brafton.com/news/youtube-overtakes-facebook-webs-biggest-social-network
9. http://wheels.blogs.nytimes.com/2012/09/25/for-tesla-motors-one-supercharger-to-bind-them/?_r=0&pagewanted=all
10. http://money.cnn.com/infographic/pf/autos/tesla-map/

CHAPTER 15

1. http://benbarry.com/project/facebooks-little-red-book
2. http://venturebeat.com/2012/06/28/gmail-hotmail-yahoo-email-users/
3. Jessica Livingstone, *Founders at Work: Stories of Startups' Early Days* (Berkeley, CA: Apress, 2008), pp. 161–62.
4. https://www.crunchbase.com/person/paul-buchheit
5. Livingstone, *Founders at Work,* p. 166.
6. Ibid., p. 165.
7. http://time.com/43263/gmail-10th-anniversary/
8. http://time.com/43263/gmail-10th-anniversary/
9. http://www.fastcompany.com/3028513/fast-feed/when-gmail-launched-on-april-1-2004-people-thought-it-was-a-joke

10. http://time.com/43263/gmail-10th-anniversary/
11. Eric Schmidt and Jonathan Rosenberg, *How Google Works* (New York: Grand Central Publishing, 2014), Kindle Edition.

APPENDIX

1. http://www.dailydot.com/business/origin-tumblr-anarchaia-projectionist-david-karp/
2. https://www.crunchbase.com/organization/tumblr; https://www.crunchbase.com/organization/posterous
3. http://observer.com/2008/01/would-you-take-a-tumblr-with-this-man/?show=all
4. https://www.linkedin.com/in/a4agarwal
5. https://www.linkedin.com/in/garrytan
6. http://www.theguardian.com/technology/2014/oct/23/tumblr-yahoo-revenues-2015-ads-nsfw
7. http://dstevenwhite.com/2011/12/29/social-media-growth-2006-2011/
8. http://www.nytimes.com/2013/05/20/technology/yahoo-to-buy-tumblr-for-1-1-billion.html?pagewanted=all
9. http://marissamayr.tumblr.com/post/50902274591/im-delighted-to-announce-that-weve-reached-an
10. http://venturebeat.com/2013/02/15/one-year-after-being-acquired-by-twitter-posterous-shuts-it-all-down/
11. http://www.nytimes.com/2011/05/08/automobiles/08TESLA.html?_r=2&emc=eta1&&pagewanted=all
12. https://www.crunchbase.com/organization/tesla-motors/funding-rounds; https://www.crunchbase.com/organization/fisker/funding-rounds
13. http://archive.fortune.com/2007/09/18/magazines/fortune/bodydoubles.fortune/index.htm
14. http://autoweek.com/article/car-news/tesla-sues-fisker-alleges-theft-trade-secrets
15. http://www.automobilemag.com/features/news/1208_q_and_a_elon_musk_ceo_tesla/fisker.html
16. http://money.cnn.com/2013/05/08/autos/tesla-earnings/
17. http://www.statista.com/statistics/272120/revenue-of-tesla/; https://gigaom.com/2013/12/09/in-case-you-still-care-fiskers-three-years-of-sales-revealed/
18. http://www.greentechmedia.com/articles/read/tesla-production-slower-than-expected-908
19. http://www.mercurynews.com/peninsula/ci_11183440
20. http://www.teslamotors.com/fi_FI/blog/tesla-motors-delivers-500th-roadster
21. http://www.autoblog.com/2011/12/16/this-is-the-last-tesla-roadster/
22. http://www.reuters.com/article/2013/06/17/us-autos-fisker-specialreport-idUSBRE95G02L20130617
23. http://techcrunch.com/2010/06/29/tesla-ipo-1-7-billion/
24. https://www.google.com/finance?cid=12607212
25. http://www.nytimes.com/aponline/2014/02/18/business/ap-us-fisker-bankruptcy.html
26. http://blog.precipice.org/why-wesabe-lost-to-mint/
27. https://www.crunchbase.com/organization/mint; https://www.crunchbase.com/organization/wesabe
28. https://www.linkedin.com/in/apatzer

29. http://mashable.com/2008/05/22/wesabe-executive-shuffl/

30. https://www.linkedin.com/in/precipice

31. http://archive.wired.com/wired/archive/8.08/comcomp_pr.html

32. http://www.netbanker.com/2008/02/400000_users_at_online_personal_finance _startups.html

33. http://www.netbanker.com/2008/02/400000_users_at_online_personal_finance _startups.html

34. http://finovate.com/bank_of_america_reports_2_million_online_personal_finance _users_of_my_portfolio/

35. http://techcrunch.com/2007/12/12/movable-type-finally-goes-open-source/

36. https://www.crunchbase.com/organization/automattic; https://www.crunchbase .com/organization/six-apart

37. http://ma.tt/2005/10/leaving-cnet/

38. http://web.archive.org/web/20060822150834/http://www.sixapart.com/about /history

39. http://readwrite.com/2006/11/20/wordpress_takes_on_sixapart

40. https://en.wordpress.com/activity/traffic/

41. http://techcrunch.com/2010/09/25/say-media-six-apart/

42. http://www.saydaily.com/2011/01/movable-type-finds-new-home-at-infocom; for full disclosure, almost one year after the sale of Movable Type to Infocom, the author's previous startup ReadWriteWeb was acquired by SAY Media to help build their tech media network while the author was currently employed as COO at ReadWriteWeb. http://readwrite.com/2011/12/13/readwriteweb_acquired_by_say_media

43. http://w3techs.com/technologies/history_overview/content_management/all/y

44. http://recode.net/2014/05/05/wordpress-parent-automattic-has-raised-160-million -now-valued-at-1-16-billion-post-money/

45. https://www.crunchbase.com/organization/youtube; https://www.crunchbase.com /organization/revver

46. https://www.crunchbase.com/person/jawed-karim

47. www.linkedin.com/pub/steven-starr/0/55/655; www.linkedin.com/pub/oliver-lucke tt/74/7a8/574; https://www.linkedin.com/in/iancjclarke48. http://www.prnewswire .com/news-releases/interactive-live-video-community—next-generation-social-net work-livevideocom-joins-forces-with-top-online-content-creator-hub-revver-5680 2212.html

49. http://techcrunch.com/2006/10/09/google-has-acquired-youtube/

50. http://www.adweek.com/news/technology/youtube-may-be-worth-40-billion-more -twitter-159861

51. https://gigaom.com/2008/02/14/liveuniverse-buys-revver-for-more-than-a-song/

52. http://techcrunch.com/2009/02/02/was-anyone-still-in-doubt-over-liveuniverses -demise/

53. https://www.crunchbase.com/organization/facebook/funding-rounds; https://www .crunchbase.com/organization/friendster

54. Noah Kagan, *How I Lost 170 Million Dollars: My Time as #30 at Facebook* (Lioncrest Publishing, 2014), Kindle Edition, p. 25.

55. http://www.inc.com/magazine/20070601/features-how-to-kill-a-great-idea.html

56. http://www.bbc.com/news/technology-11738925

57. http://mashable.com/2014/02/03/jonathan-abrams-friendster-facebook/

58. https://www.crunchbase.com/organization/linkedin; https://www.crunchbase.com /organization/spoke

59. https://www.linkedin.com/in/reidhoffman

60. https://www.linkedin.com/static?key=founders

61. http://www.bizjournals.com/sanjose/stories/2003/04/21/daily45.html

62. https://www.linkedin.com/in/bentsmith4

63. https://ourstory.linkedin.com/

64. Jessica Livingstone, *Founders at Work: Stories of Startups' Early Days* (Berkeley, CA: Apress, 2008).

65. http://www.bizjournals.com/triad/stories/2002/01/07/editorial1.html?page=all; http://www.marketwatch.com/story/juno-ipo-announcement-follows-65-million -private-placement; http://www.referenceforbusiness.com/history2/21/Juno-Online -Services-Inc.html

66. Brad Stone, *The Everything Store: Jeff Bezos and the Age of Amazon* (New York: Little, Brown and Company, 2013).

67. Livingstone, *Founders at Work;* http://www.referenceforbusiness.com/history2/21 /Juno-Online-Services-Inc.html; http://www.bizjournals.com/triad/stories/2002/01 /07/editorial1.html?page=all

68. http://news.cnet.com/NetZero,-Juno-to-unite-in-merger/2100-1033_3-268057.html

69. http://venturebeat.com/2011/07/22/cvent-reggie-aggarwal-funding/; http://www.bu sinesstravelnews.com/Business-Travel-Agencies/OnVantage,-StarCite-To-Merge /?ida=Technology&a=mgmt

70. https://www.linkedin.com/in/reggieaggarwal

71. http://www.cvent.com/en/company/management-team.shtml

72. https://www.linkedin.com/in/tgkramer

73. www.linkedin.com/pub/john-pino/7/a25/692/en

74. http://www.forbes.com/sites/tomiogeron/2013/08/09/cvent-shares-soar-after-ipo -for-event-planning/

75. http://www.bizjournals.com/philadelphia/news/2012/01/05/active-network-pur chases-icg-group.html

76. http://www.referenceforbusiness.com/history2/56/McDonald-s-Corporation.html

77. Ray Kroc, *Grinding It Out: The Making of McDonald's* (Chicago: Contemporary Books, 1977), p. 6.

78. http://www.fundinguniverse.com/company-histories/white-castle-system-inc -history/

79. http://www.referenceforbusiness.com/history2/40/White-Castle-System-Inc.html

80. John F. Love, *McDonald's: Behind the Arches* (New York: Bantam Books, 1995), p. 3.

81. https://www.crunchbase.com/organization/google

82. https://www.google.com/intl/en-GB/about/company/

83. www.internetlivestats.com/google-search-statistics/

84. http://www.internetlivestats.com/google-search-statistics/

85. http://finance.yahoo.com/q?s=GOOG

86. https://www.crunchbase.com/organization/PayPal

87. http://www.gadgetdetail.com/history-paypal; http://ecorner.stanford.edu/authorMa terialInfo.html?mid=1031

88. https://www.crunchbase.com/organization/DropBox

89. http://ecorner.stanford.edu/authorMaterialInfo.html?mid=2986

90. http://www.referralsaasquatch.com/dropbox-customer-referral-program-by-the -numbers/

91. https://www.crunchbase.com/organization/AirBnB

92. http://notes.fundersandfounders.com/post/82297315548/how-airbnb-started

93. https://growthhackers.com/companies/airbnb/
94. http://newsroom.uber.com/2010/12/ubers-founding/
95. https://growthhackers.com/companies/uber/
96. http://www.slashgear.com/uber-expands-55-of-us-population-now-covered-2834
    3251/; http://www.forbes.com/sites/briansolomon/2015/05/01/the-numbers-behind
    -ubers-exploding-driver-force/
97. https://www.crunchbase.com/organization/Twitter
98. http://mashable.com/2009/01/09/twitter-growth-2008/

INDEX